COLLECTION EDITOR: **JENNIFER GRÜNWALD**
ASSISTANT EDITOR: **SARAH BRUNSTAD**
ASSOCIATE MANAGING EDITOR: **ALEX STARBUCK**
EDITOR, SPECIAL PROJECTS: **MARK D. BEAZLEY**
SENIOR EDITOR, SPECIAL PROJECTS: **JEFF YOUNGQUIST**
SVP PRINT, SALES & MARKETING: **DAVID GABRIEL**
BOOK DESIGN: **JEFF POWELL**

EDITOR IN CHIEF: **AXEL ALONSO**
CHIEF CREATIVE OFFICER: **JOE QUESADA**
PUBLISHER: **DAN BUCKLEY**
EXECUTIVE PRODUCER: **ALAN FINE**

NEW AVENGERS VOL. 3: OTHER WORLDS. Contains material originally published in magazine form as NEW AVENGERS #13.INH and #14-17. First printing 2014. ISBN# 978-0-7851-5484-6. Published by MARVEL WORLDWIDE, INC., a subsidiary of MARVEL ENTERTAINMENT, LLC. OFFICE OF PUBLICATION: 135 West 50th Street, New York, NY 10020. Copyright © 2013 and 2014 Marvel Characters, Inc. All rights reserved. All characters featured in this issue and the distinctive names and likenesses thereof, and all related indicia are trademarks of Marvel Characters, Inc. No similarity between any of the names, characters, persons, and/or institutions in this magazine with those of any living or dead person or institution is intended, and any such similarity which may exist is purely coincidental. **Printed in the U.S.A.** ALAN FINE, EVP - Office of the President, Marvel Worldwide, Inc. and EVP & CMO Marvel Characters B.V.; DAN BUCKLEY, Publisher & President - Print, Animation & Digital Divisions; JOE QUESADA, Chief Creative Officer; TOM BREVOORT, SVP of Publishing; DAVID BOGART, SVP of Operations & Procurement, Publishing; C.B. CEBULSKI, SVP of Creator & Content Development; DAVID GABRIEL, SVP Print, Sales & Marketing; JIM O'KEEFE, VP of Operations & Logistics; DAN CARR, Executive Director of Publishing Technology; SUSAN CRESPI, Editorial Operations Manager; ALEX MORALES, Publishing Operations Manager; STAN LEE, Chairman Emeritus. For information regarding advertising in Marvel Comics or on Marvel.com, please contact Niza Disla, Director of Marvel Partnerships, at ndisla@marvel.com. For Marvel subscription inquiries, please call 800-217-9158. **Manufactured between 4/25/2014 and 6/9/2014 by R.R. DONNELLEY, INC., SALEM, VA, USA.**

10 9 8 7 6 5 4 3 2 1

WRITER: **JONATHAN HICKMAN**

ISSUES #13-15

ARTIST: **SIMONE BIANCHI**

INK & INKWASH: **SIMONE BIANCHI & RICCARDO PIERUCCINI**

COLOR ARTIST: **ADRIANO DALL'ALPI**

COVER ART: **SIMONE BIANCHI**

ISSUES #16-17

ARTIST: **RAGS MORALES**

COLOR ARTIST: **FRANK MARTIN**

COVER ART: **MIKE DEODATO & FRANK MARTIN (#16)** AND **LEINIL FRANCIS YU & DAVID CURIEL (#17)**

LETTERER: **VC'S JOE CARAMAGNA**

ASSISTANT EDITOR: **JAKE THOMAS**

EDITORS: **TOM BREVOORT** WITH **LAUREN SANKOVITCH & WIL MOSS**

EVERYTHING DIES. YOU. ME. EVERYONE ON THIS PLANET. IT'S INEVITABLE, AND I HAVE COME TO ACCEPT IT. WHAT I FIND *UNACCEPTABLE* IS THE UNNATURAL ACCELERATION OF THAT END.

ON AN ALTERNATE EARTH AN EVENT OCCURRED THAT CAUSED THE EARLY DEATH OF A UNIVERSE. THIS CAUSED A TINY CONTRACTION, SMASHING TWO UNIVERSES TOGETHER AT THE INCURSION POINT OF THE INITIAL EVENT.

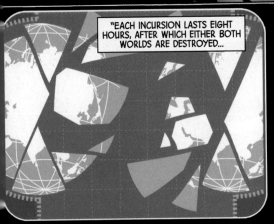

"EACH INCURSION LASTS EIGHT HOURS, AFTER WHICH EITHER BOTH WORLDS ARE DESTROYED...

"...OR ONLY ONE EARTH IS SACRIFICED, SPARING BOTH UNIVERSES.

"WE SHOULD BE ABLE TO DETECT THE INCURSIONS, SO AT LEAST WE'LL KNOW WHEN ONE IS COMING. HOWEVER...

"...INFINITE WORLDS, INFINITE OUTCOMES. IF THIS COULD EASILY BE STOPPED, IT SHOULD HAVE BEEN STOPPED."

BLACK SWAN, YOU JUMPED HERE FROM ANOTHER WORLD, DESTROYING THE PLANET YOU CAME FROM.

THE TURN OF THE WHEEL BREAKS HOPE, CRUSHES WHAT MAKES US DECENT AND STEALS WHAT HONOR REMAINS.

WE WILL TRY EVERY GOOD AND RIGHTEOUS SOLUTION WE CAN.

AND IF THOSE DON'T WORK...?

THE ILLUMINATI

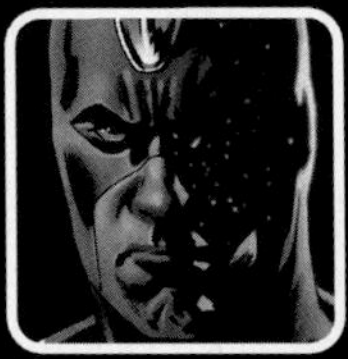
BLACK BOLT
Celestial Messiah

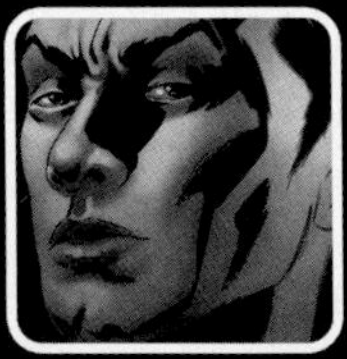
NAMOR
Imperius Rex

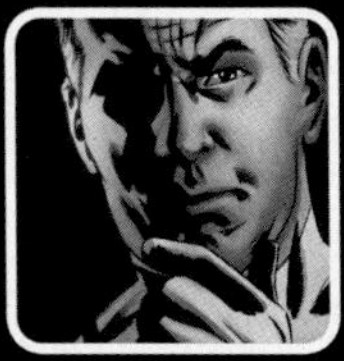
REED RICHARDS
Universal Builder

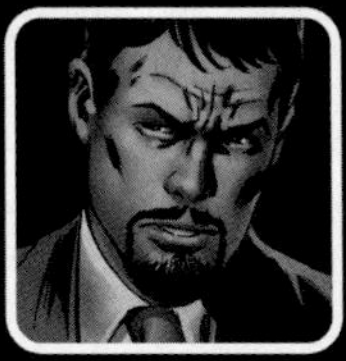
IRON MAN
Master of Machines

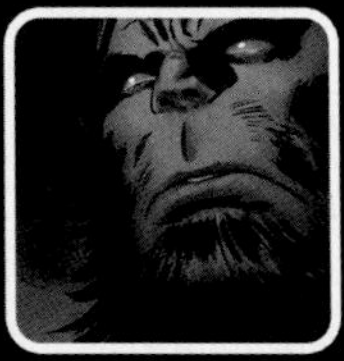
BEAST
Hero of Legend

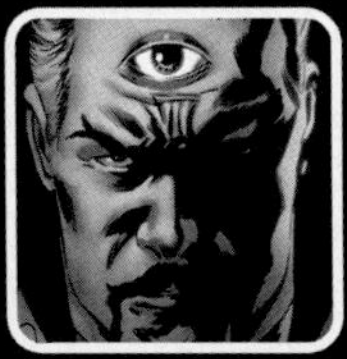
DOCTOR STRANGE
Sorcerer Supreme

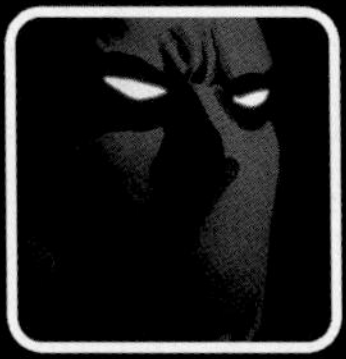
BLACK PANTHER
King of the Dead

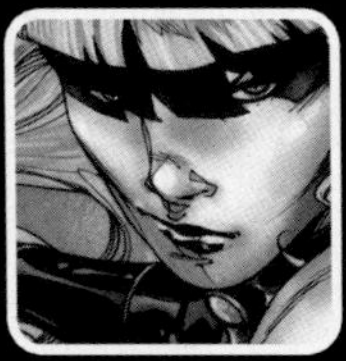
BLACK SWAN
Incursion Survivor

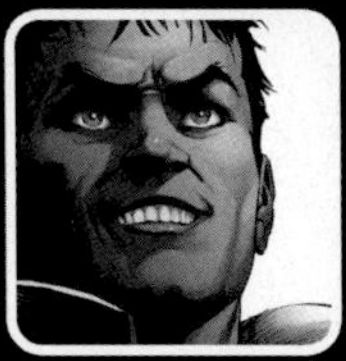
MAXIMUS
Inhuman Madman

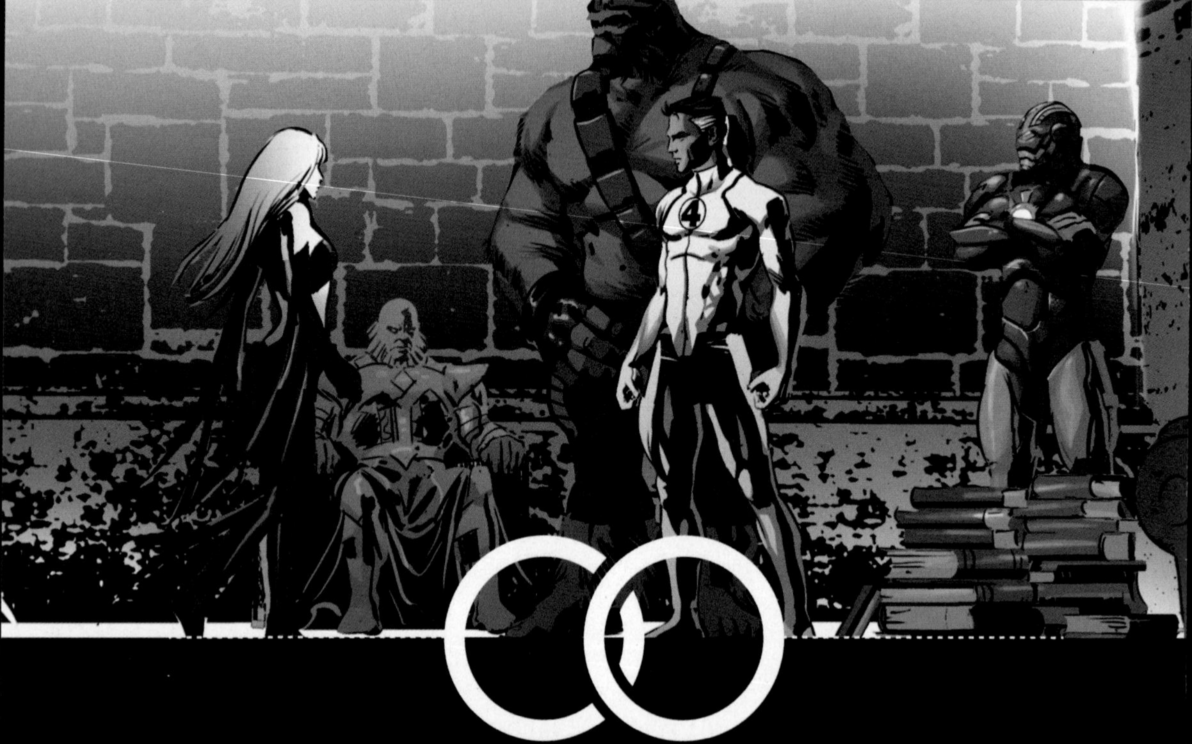

THE WORLD CHANGED OVERNIGHT AS THE GREAT MACHINE CAUSED CASCADING GLOBAL TERRIGENESIS.

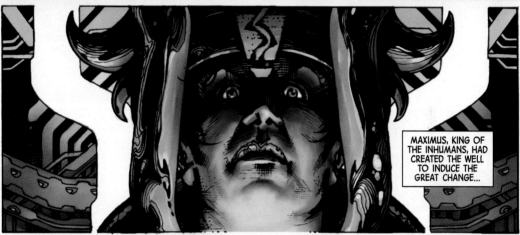

MAXIMUS, KING OF THE INHUMANS, HAD CREATED THE WELL TO INDUCE THE GREAT CHANGE...

AND TO USHER IN A NEW DAY FOR HIS EXPANDING KINGDOM.

THE ROYAL FAMILY WATCHED AS ALL THE UNCHANGED-- THE LOST TRIBES AND THE HIDDEN ONES--BEGAN TO METAMORPHOSE AS THE MIST--THE TRANSFORMATIVE FALLOUT--SPREAD ACROSS THE GLOBE.

IT SHOULD HAVE BEEN THE START OF A NEW INHUMAN AGE.

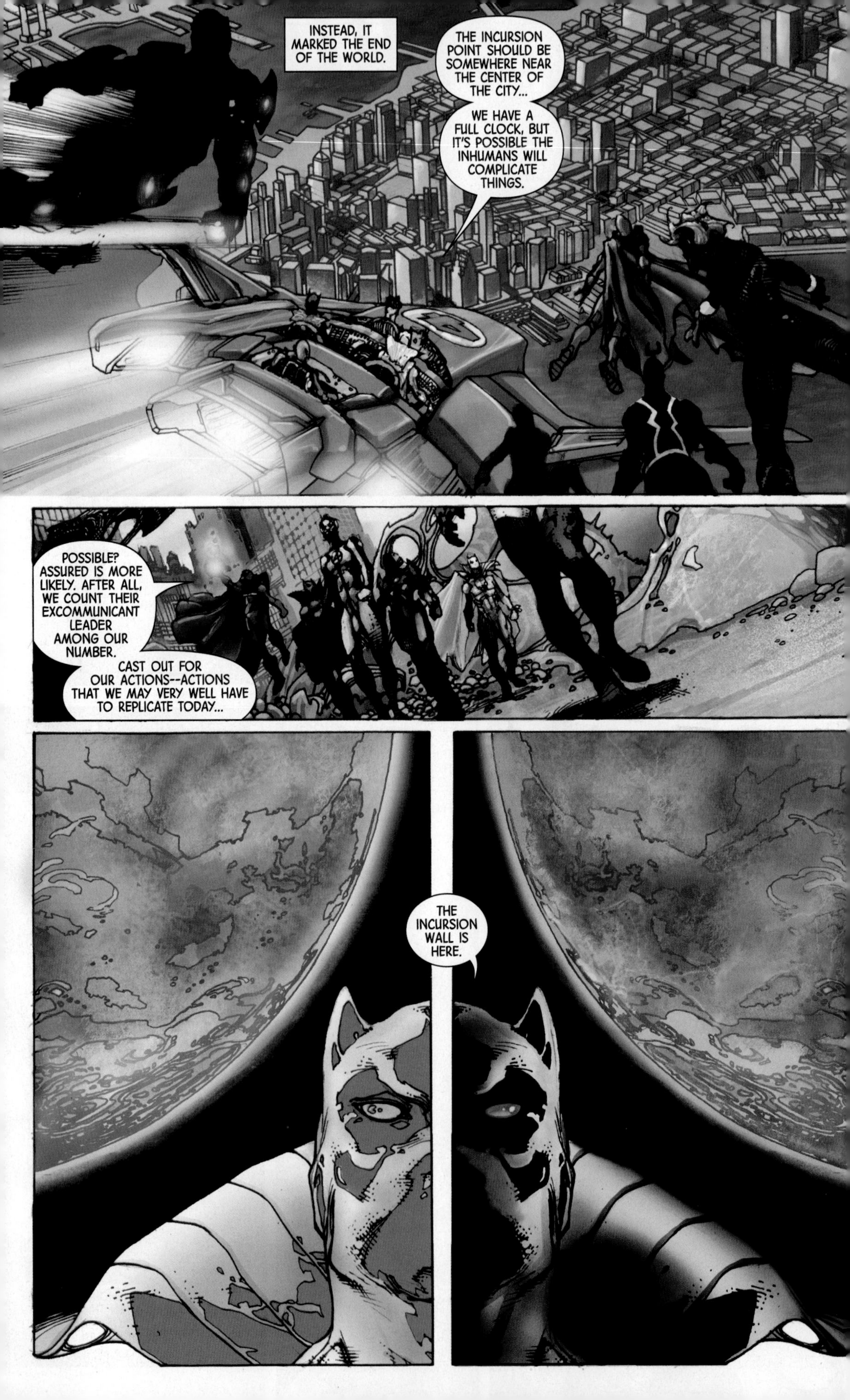
INSTEAD, IT MARKED THE END OF THE WORLD.
THE INCURSION POINT SHOULD BE SOMEWHERE NEAR THE CENTER OF THE CITY...
WE HAVE A FULL CLOCK, BUT IT'S POSSIBLE THE INHUMANS WILL COMPLICATE THINGS.
POSSIBLE? ASSURED IS MORE LIKELY. AFTER ALL, WE COUNT THEIR EXCOMMUNICANT LEADER AMONG OUR NUMBER.
CAST OUT FOR OUR ACTIONS--ACTIONS THAT WE MAY VERY WELL HAVE TO REPLICATE TODAY...
THE INCURSION WALL IS HERE.

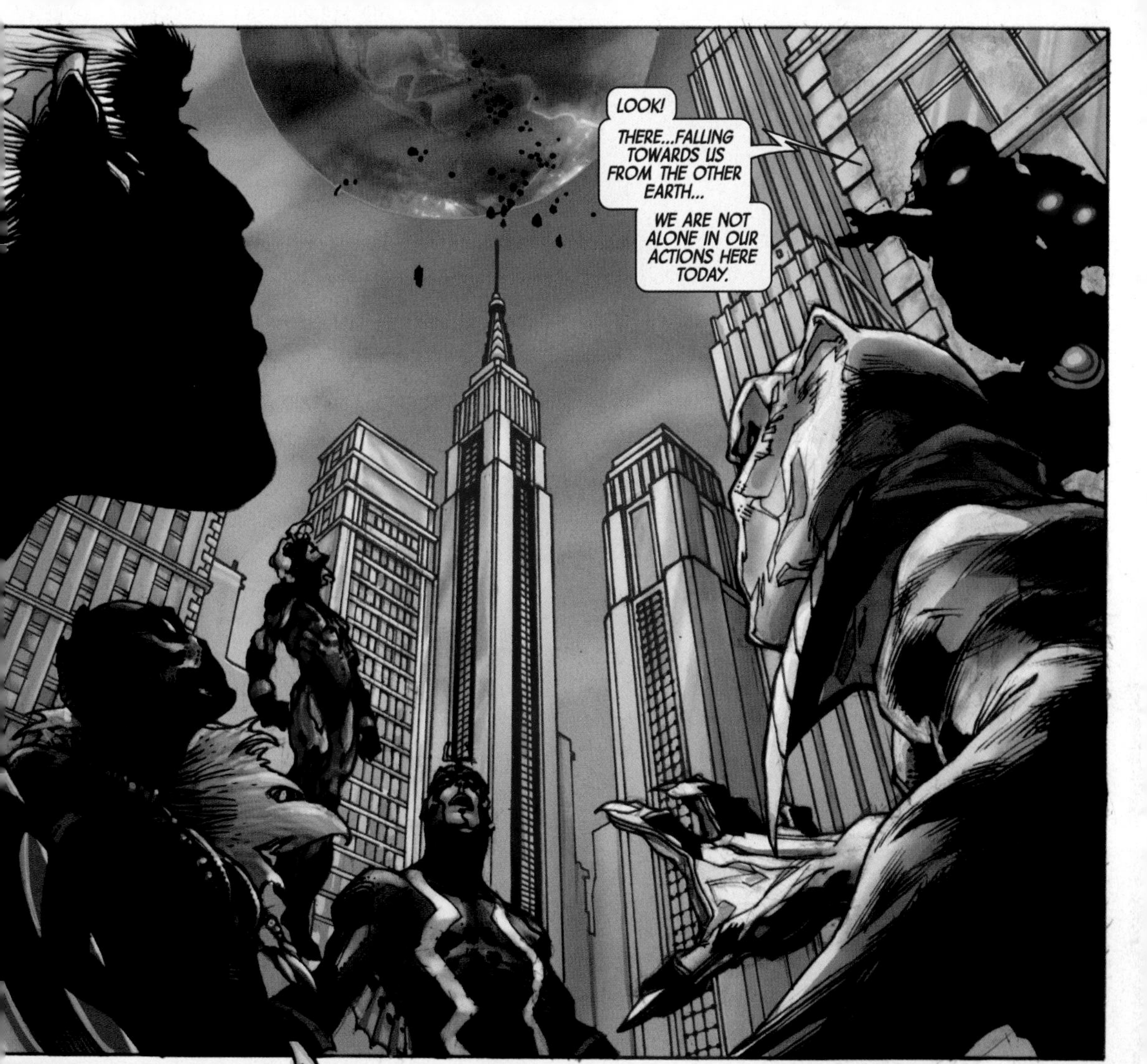
LOOK!
THERE...FALLING TOWARDS US FROM THE OTHER EARTH...
WE ARE NOT ALONE IN OUR ACTIONS HERE TODAY.

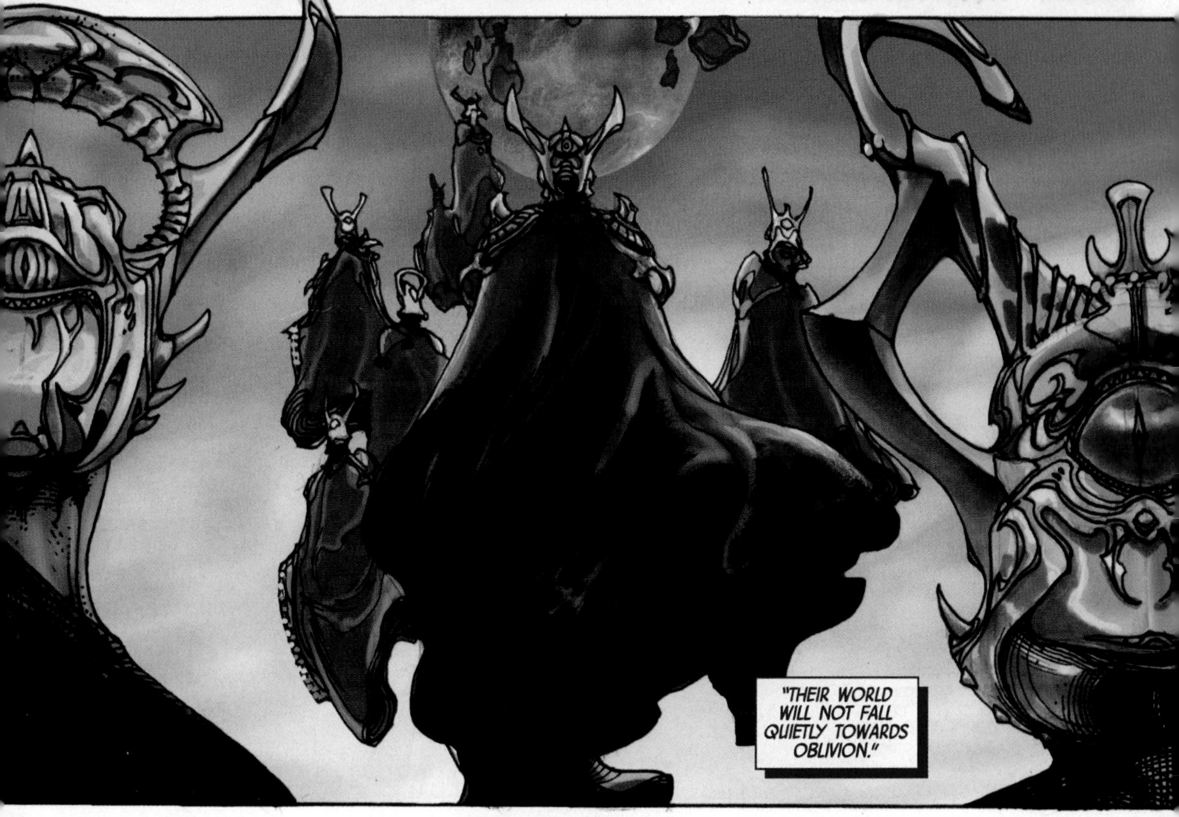
"THEIR WORLD WILL NOT FALL QUIETLY TOWARDS OBLIVION."

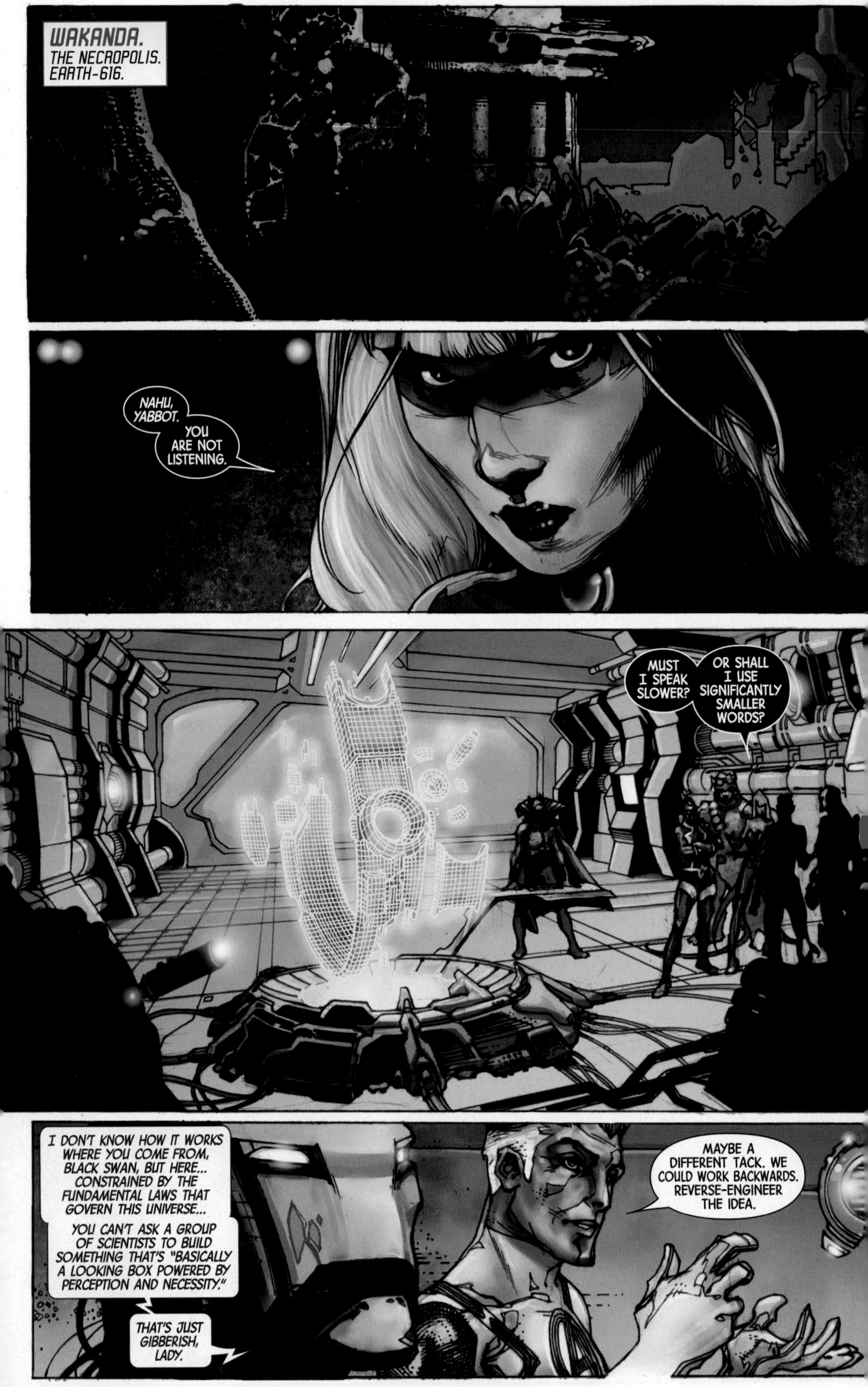
WAKANDA.
THE NECROPOLIS.
EARTH-616.
NAHU, YABBOT.
YOU ARE NOT LISTENING.
MUST I SPEAK SLOWER?
OR SHALL I USE SIGNIFICANTLY SMALLER WORDS?
I DON'T KNOW HOW IT WORKS WHERE YOU COME FROM, BLACK SWAN, BUT HERE... CONSTRAINED BY THE FUNDAMENTAL LAWS THAT GOVERN THIS UNIVERSE...
YOU CAN'T ASK A GROUP OF SCIENTISTS TO BUILD SOMETHING THAT'S "BASICALLY A LOOKING BOX POWERED BY PERCEPTION AND NECESSITY."
THAT'S JUST GIBBERISH, LADY.
MAYBE A DIFFERENT TACK. WE COULD WORK BACKWARDS. REVERSE-ENGINEER THE IDEA.

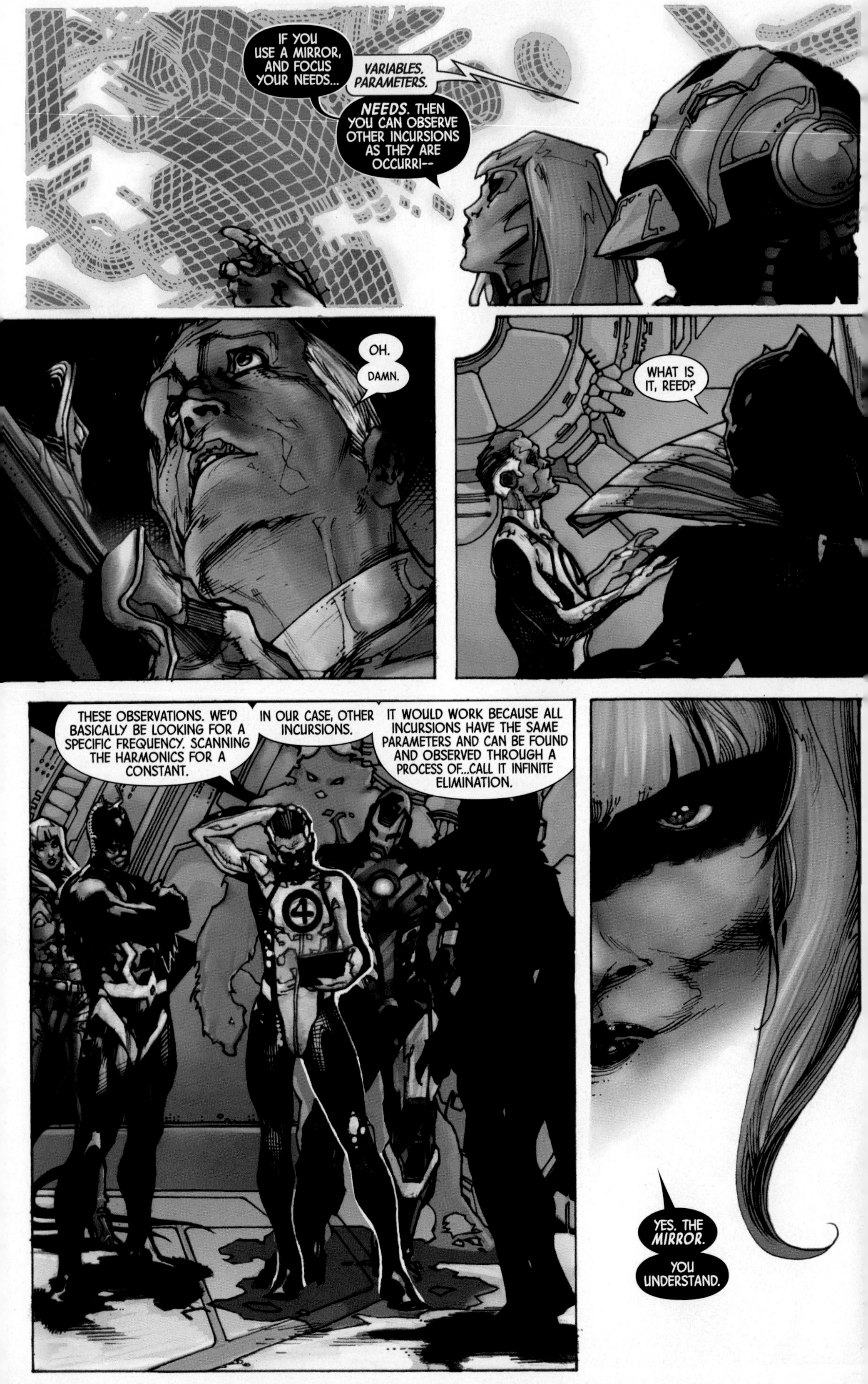
IF YOU USE A MIRROR, AND FOCUS YOUR NEEDS...
VARIABLES. PARAMETERS.
NEEDS. THEN YOU CAN OBSERVE OTHER INCURSIONS AS THEY ARE OCCURRI--
OH.
DAMN.
WHAT IS IT, REED?
THESE OBSERVATIONS. WE'D BASICALLY BE LOOKING FOR A SPECIFIC FREQUENCY. SCANNING THE HARMONICS FOR A CONSTANT.
IN OUR CASE, OTHER INCURSIONS.
IT WOULD WORK BECAUSE ALL INCURSIONS HAVE THE SAME PARAMETERS AND CAN BE FOUND AND OBSERVED THROUGH A PROCESS OF...CALL IT INFINITE ELIMINATION.
YES. THE MIRROR.
YOU UNDERSTAND.

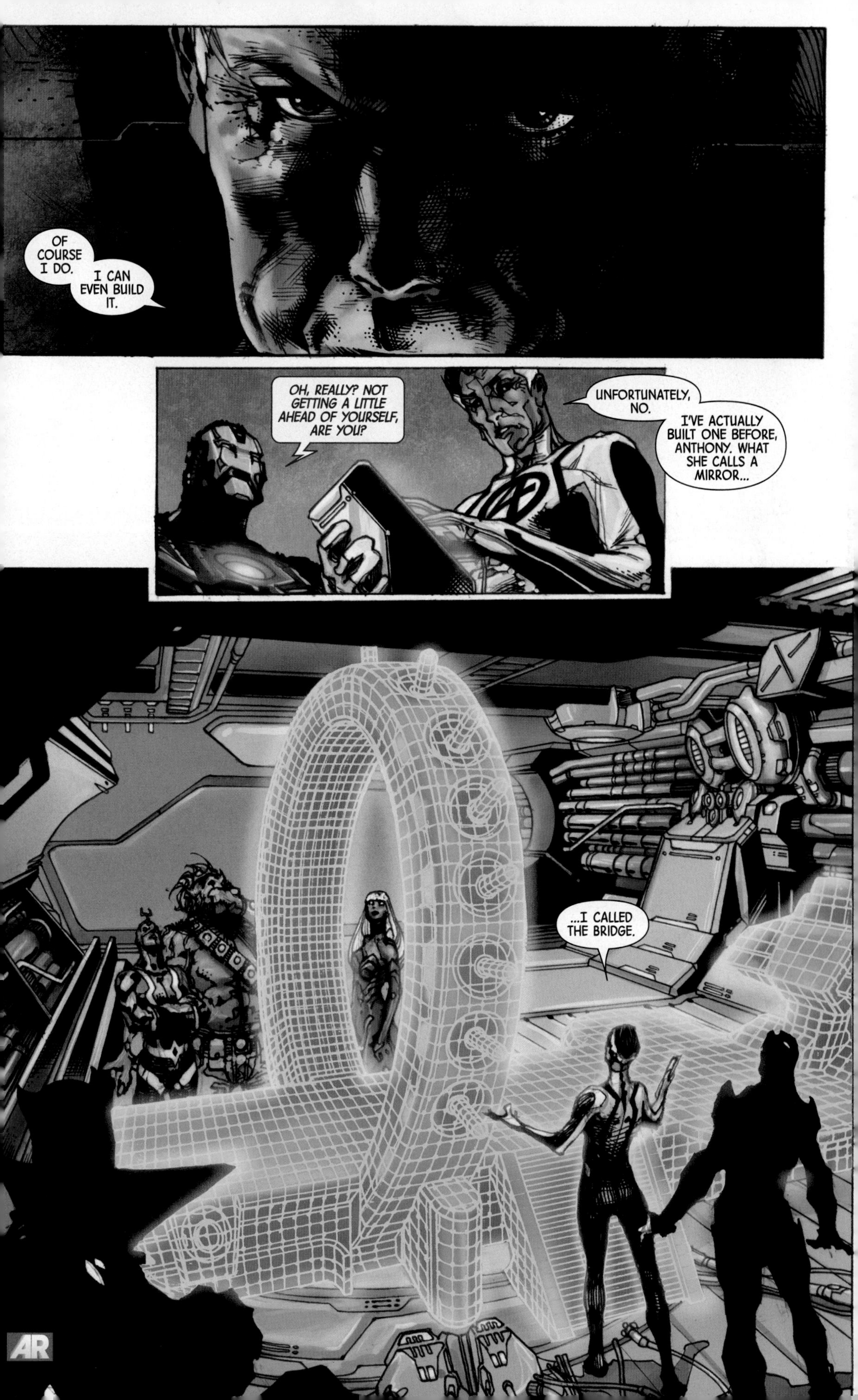
OF COURSE I DO.
I CAN EVEN BUILD IT.
OH, REALLY? NOT GETTING A LITTLE AHEAD OF YOURSELF, ARE YOU?
UNFORTUNATELY, NO.
I'VE ACTUALLY BUILT ONE BEFORE, ANTHONY. WHAT SHE CALLS A MIRROR...
...I CALLED THE BRIDGE.

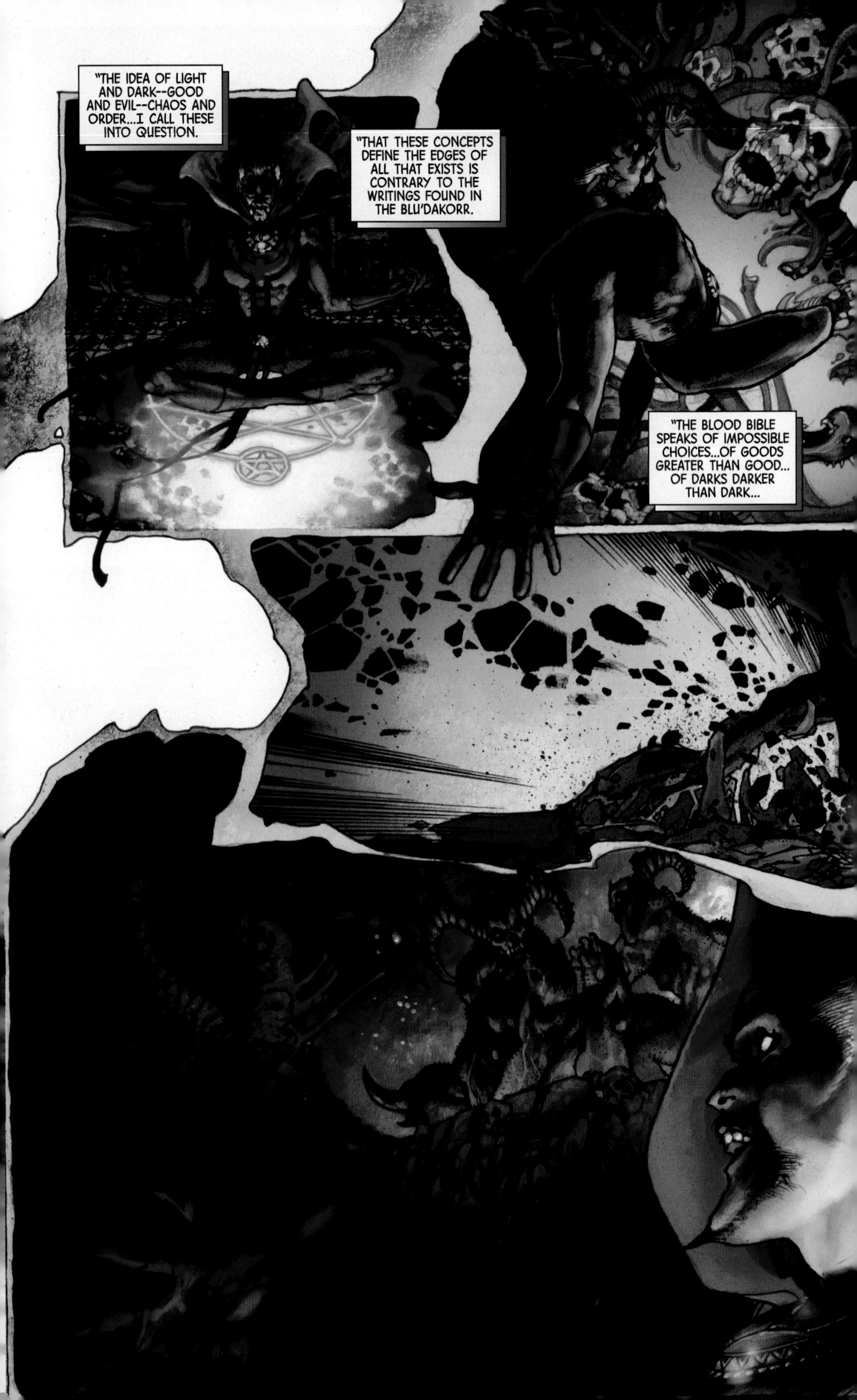
"THE IDEA OF LIGHT AND DARK--GOOD AND EVIL--CHAOS AND ORDER...I CALL THESE INTO QUESTION.
"THAT THESE CONCEPTS DEFINE THE EDGES OF ALL THAT EXISTS IS CONTRARY TO THE WRITINGS FOUND IN THE BLU'DAKORR.
"THE BLOOD BIBLE SPEAKS OF IMPOSSIBLE CHOICES...OF GOODS GREATER THAN GOOD... OF DARKS DARKER THAN DARK...

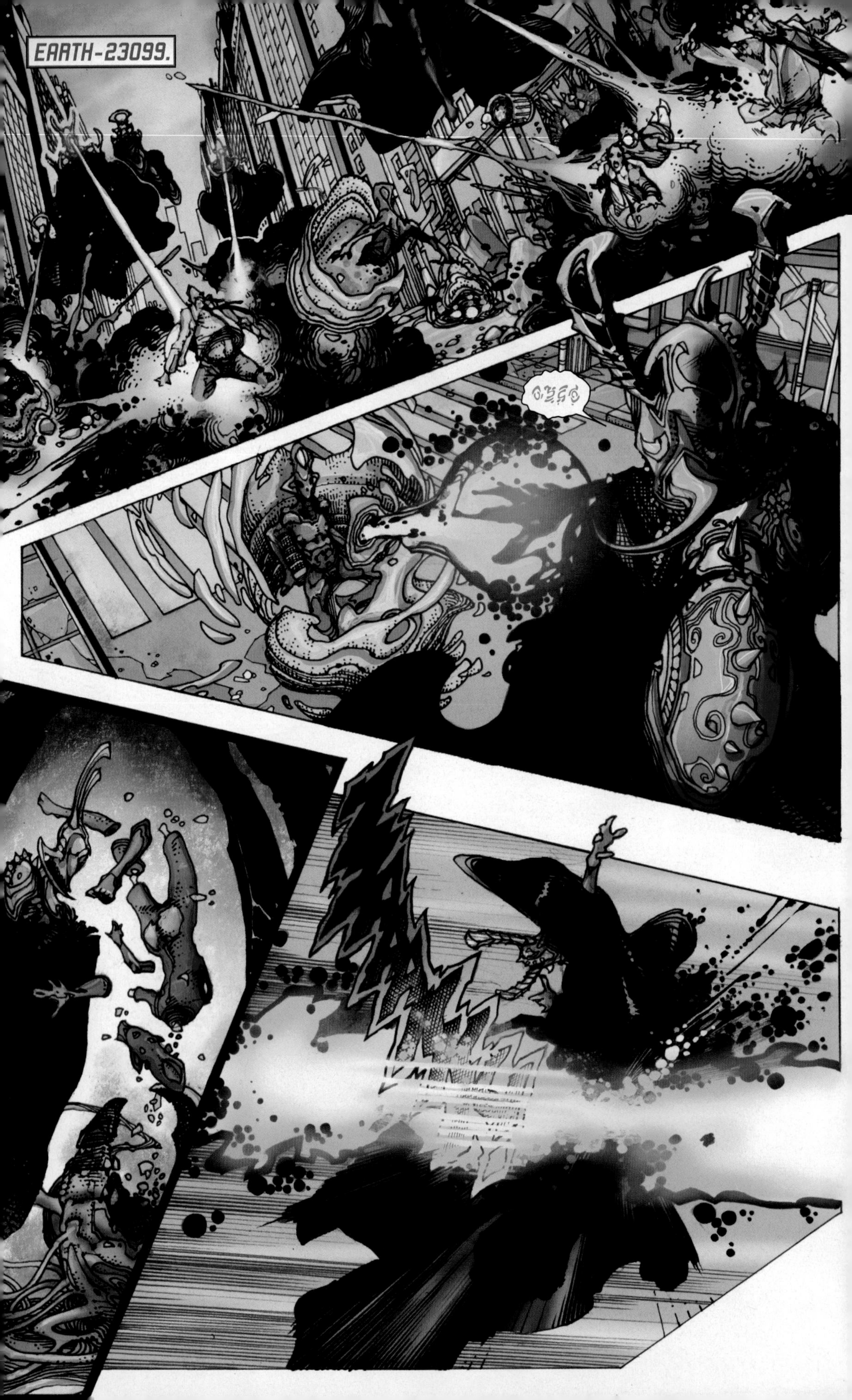
EARTH-23099.

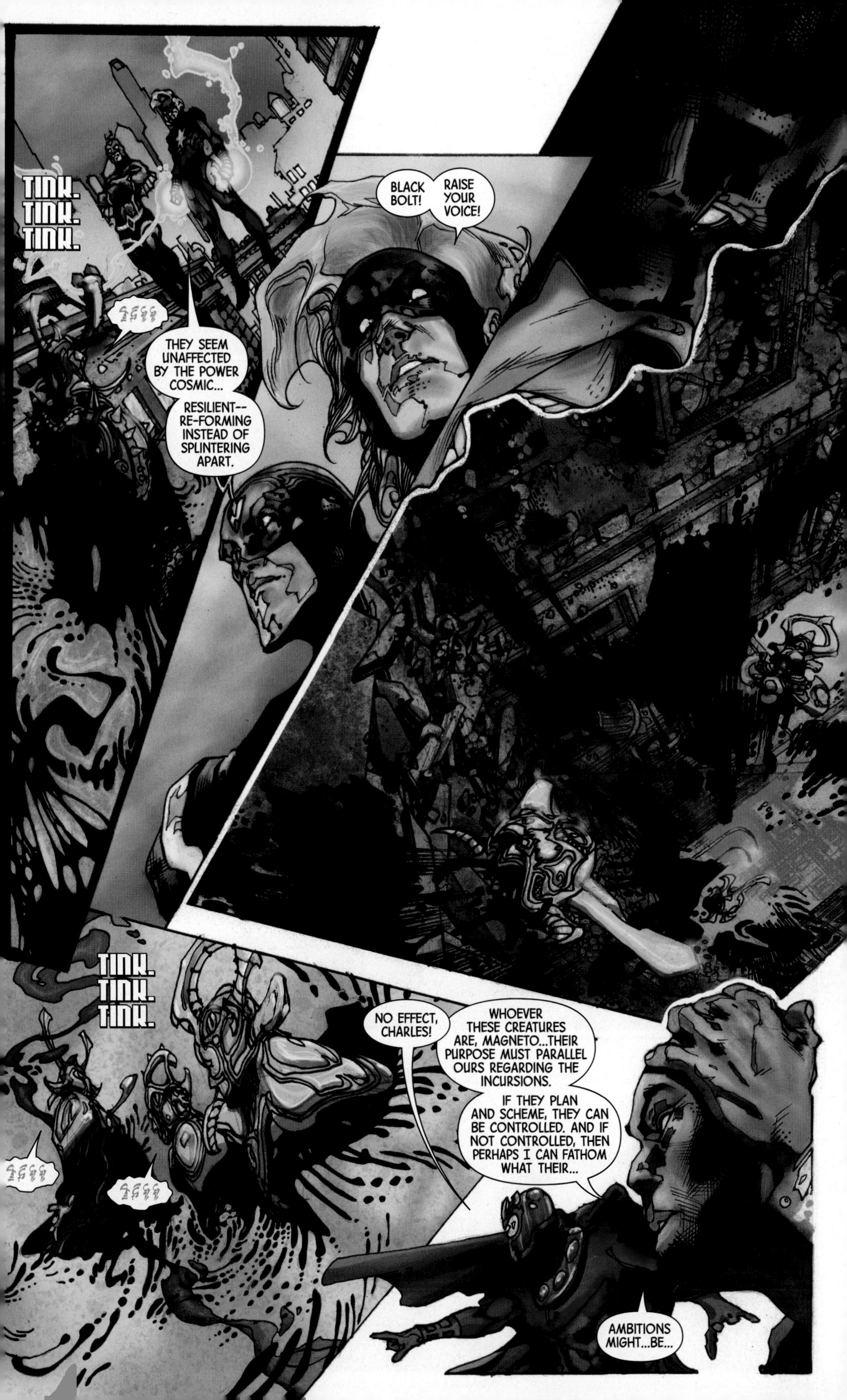
TINK.
TINK.
TINK.
THEY SEEM UNAFFECTED BY THE POWER COSMIC...
RESILIENT-- RE-FORMING INSTEAD OF SPLINTERING APART.
BLACK BOLT!
RAISE YOUR VOICE!
TINK.
TINK.
TINK.
NO EFFECT, CHARLES!
WHOEVER THESE CREATURES ARE, MAGNETO...THEIR PURPOSE MUST PARALLEL OURS REGARDING THE INCURSIONS.
IF THEY PLAN AND SCHEME, THEY CAN BE CONTROLLED. AND IF NOT CONTROLLED, THEN PERHAPS I CAN FATHOM WHAT THEIR...
AMBITIONS MIGHT...BE...

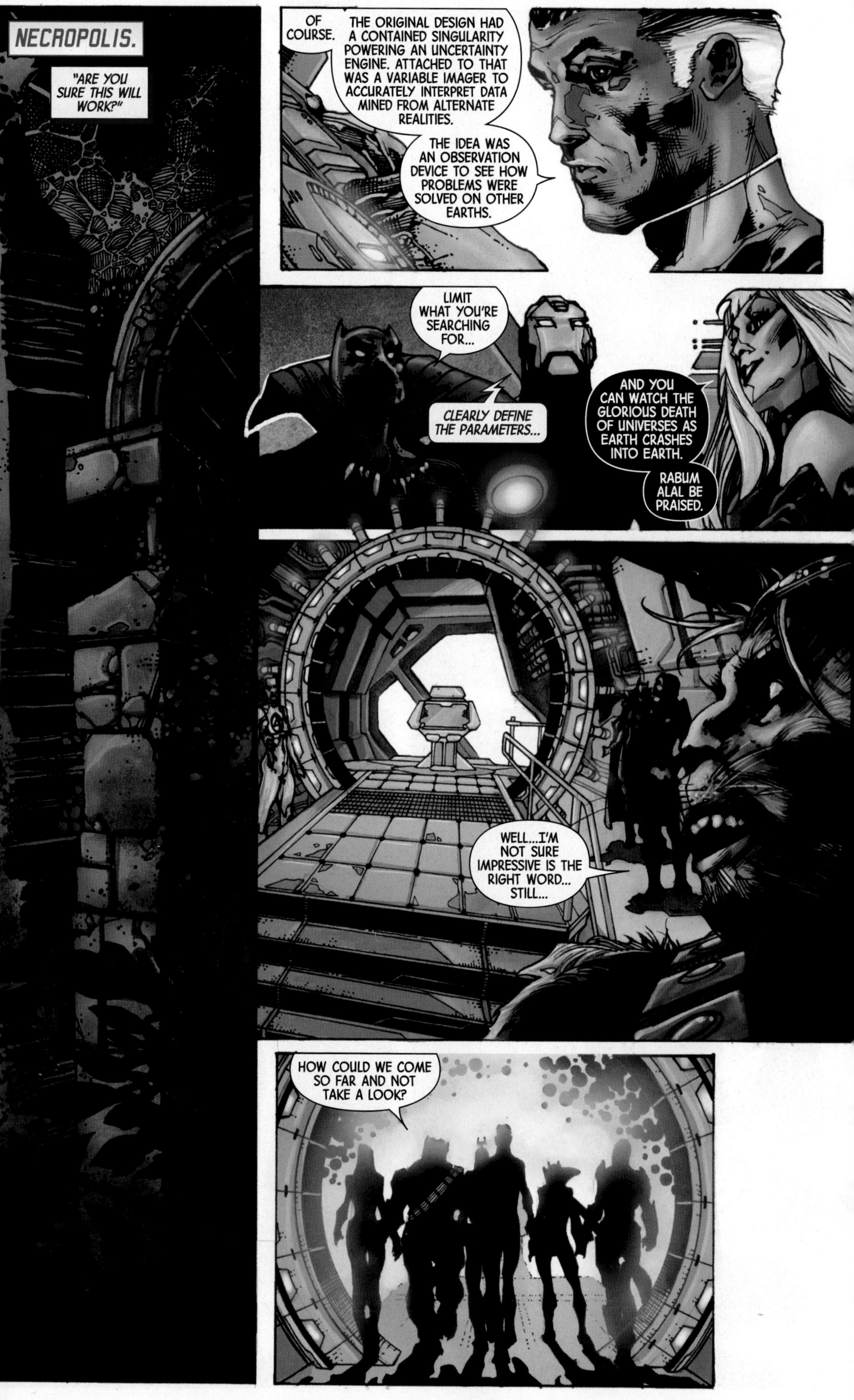
NECROPOLIS.
"ARE YOU SURE THIS WILL WORK?"
OF COURSE.
THE ORIGINAL DESIGN HAD A CONTAINED SINGULARITY POWERING AN UNCERTAINTY ENGINE. ATTACHED TO THAT WAS A VARIABLE IMAGER TO ACCURATELY INTERPRET DATA MINED FROM ALTERNATE REALITIES.
THE IDEA WAS AN OBSERVATION DEVICE TO SEE HOW PROBLEMS WERE SOLVED ON OTHER EARTHS.
LIMIT WHAT YOU'RE SEARCHING FOR...
CLEARLY DEFINE THE PARAMETERS...
AND YOU CAN WATCH THE GLORIOUS DEATH OF UNIVERSES AS EARTH CRASHES INTO EARTH.
RABUM ALAL BE PRAISED.
WELL...I'M NOT SURE IMPRESSIVE IS THE RIGHT WORD... STILL...
HOW COULD WE COME SO FAR AND NOT TAKE A LOOK?

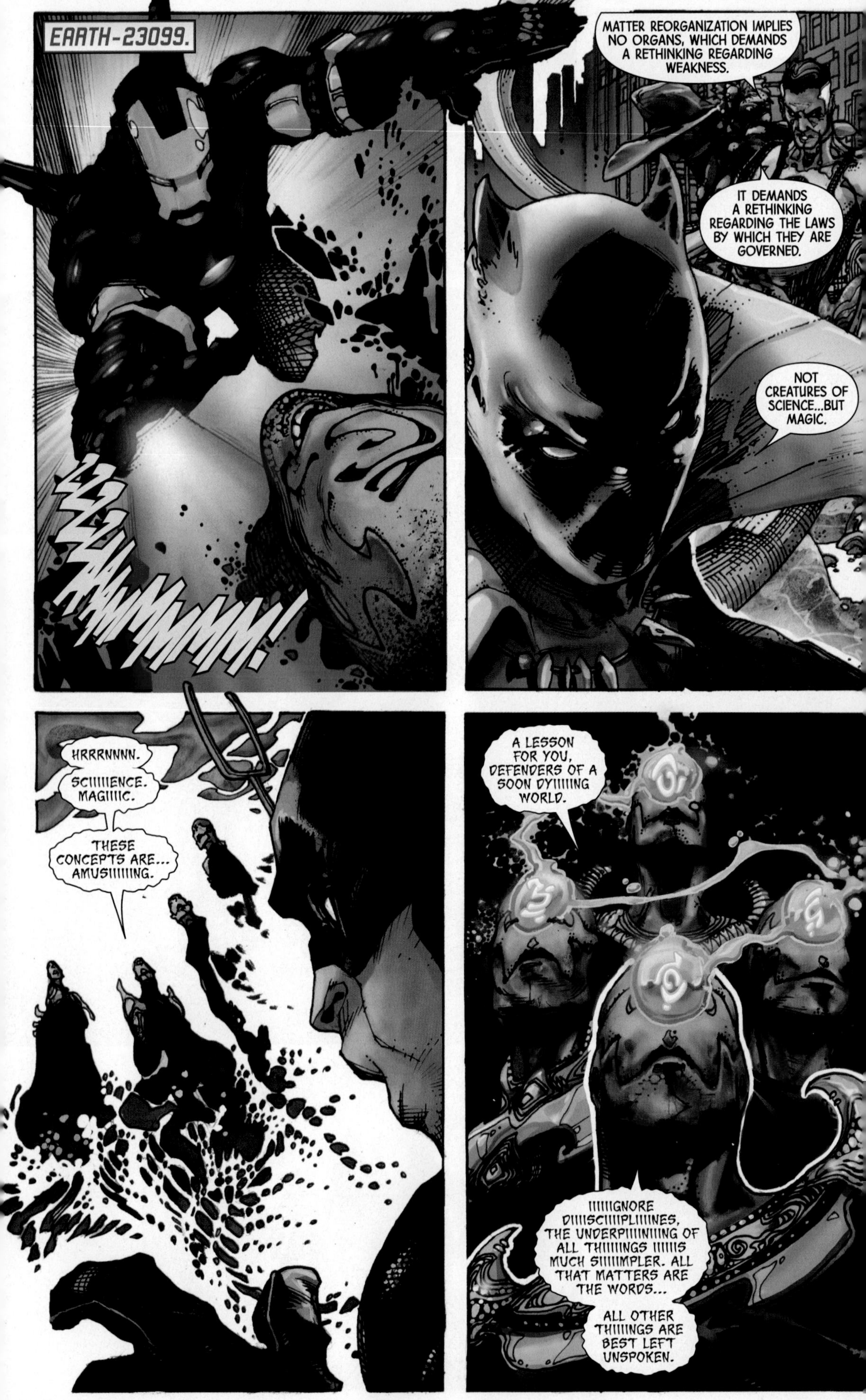
EARTH-23099.
ZZZZWHMMMM!
MATTER REORGANIZATION IMPLIES NO ORGANS, WHICH DEMANDS A RETHINKING REGARDING WEAKNESS.
IT DEMANDS A RETHINKING REGARDING THE LAWS BY WHICH THEY ARE GOVERNED.
NOT CREATURES OF SCIENCE...BUT MAGIC.
HRRRNNNN.
SCIIIIIENCE. MAGIIIIC.
THESE CONCEPTS ARE... AMUSIIIIIING.
A LESSON FOR YOU, DEFENDERS OF A SOON DYIIIIING WORLD.
IIIIIIGNORE DIIIISCIIIIPLIIIINES, THE UNDERPIIIINIIIING OF ALL THIIIINGS IIIIIIS MUCH SIIIIIMPLER. ALL THAT MATTERS ARE THE WORDS...
ALL OTHER THIIIINGS ARE BEST LEFT UNSPOKEN.

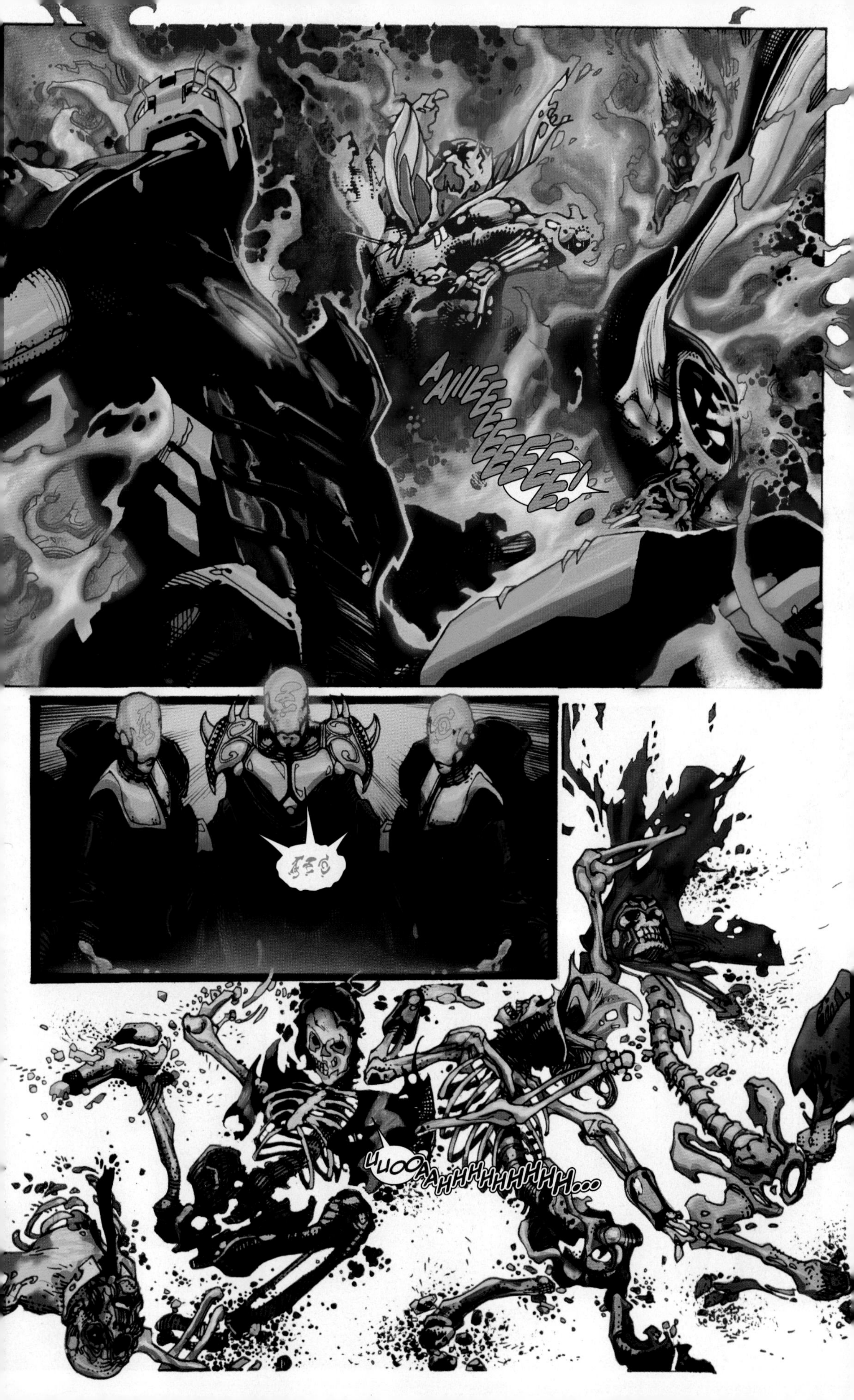
AIIIEEEEEEEEE!
UUOOAAHHHHHHHHH...

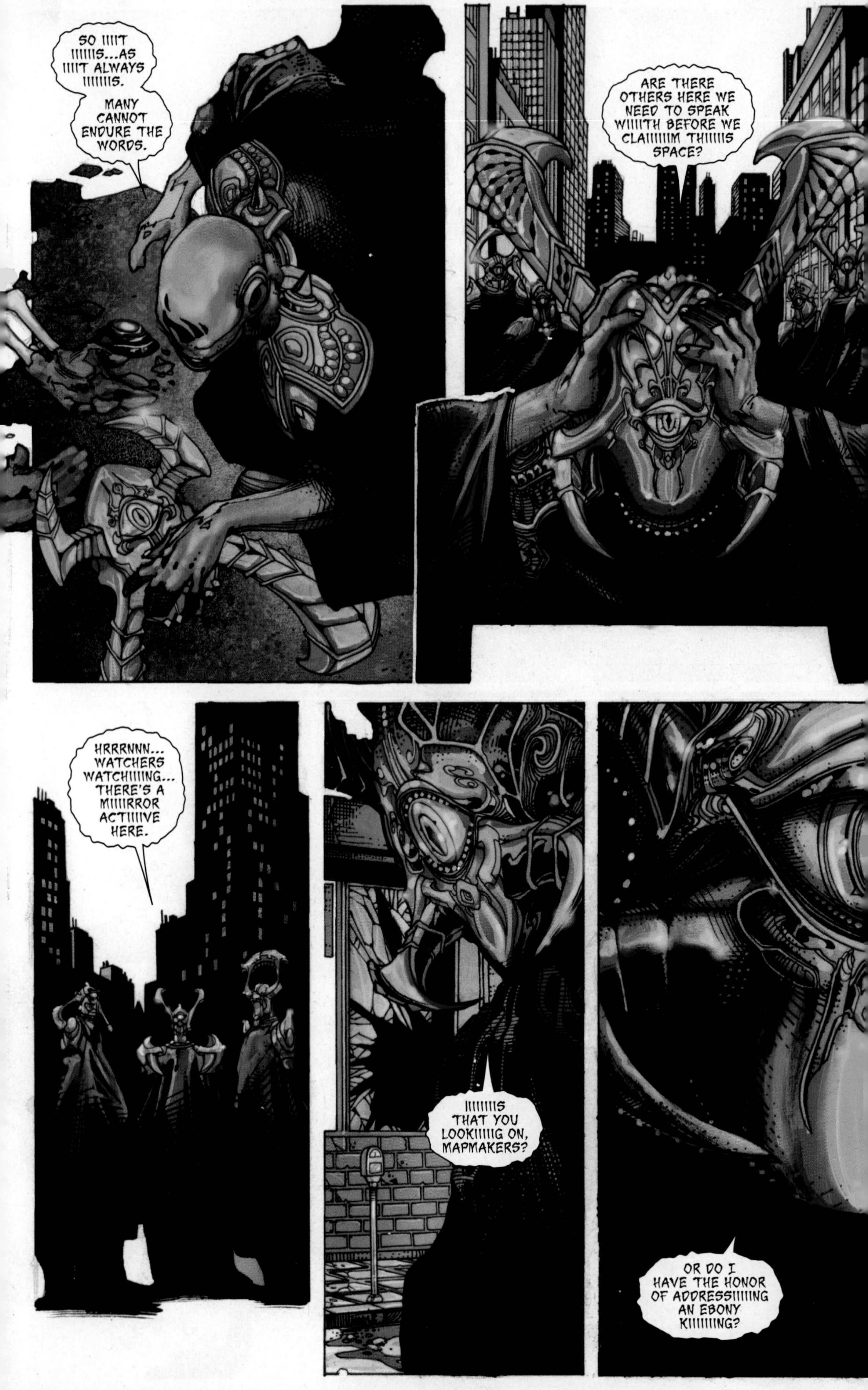
SO IIIIT IIIIIIS...AS IIIIT ALWAYS IIIIIIIS.
MANY CANNOT ENDURE THE WORDS.
ARE THERE OTHERS HERE WE NEED TO SPEAK WIIIITH BEFORE WE CLAIIIIIM THIIIIIS SPACE?
HRRRNNN... WATCHERS WATCHIIIING... THERE'S A MIIIIRROR ACTIIIIVE HERE.
IIIIIIIS THAT YOU LOOKIIIIIG ON, MAPMAKERS?
OR DO I HAVE THE HONOR OF ADDRESSIIIIIING AN EBONY KIIIIIIING?

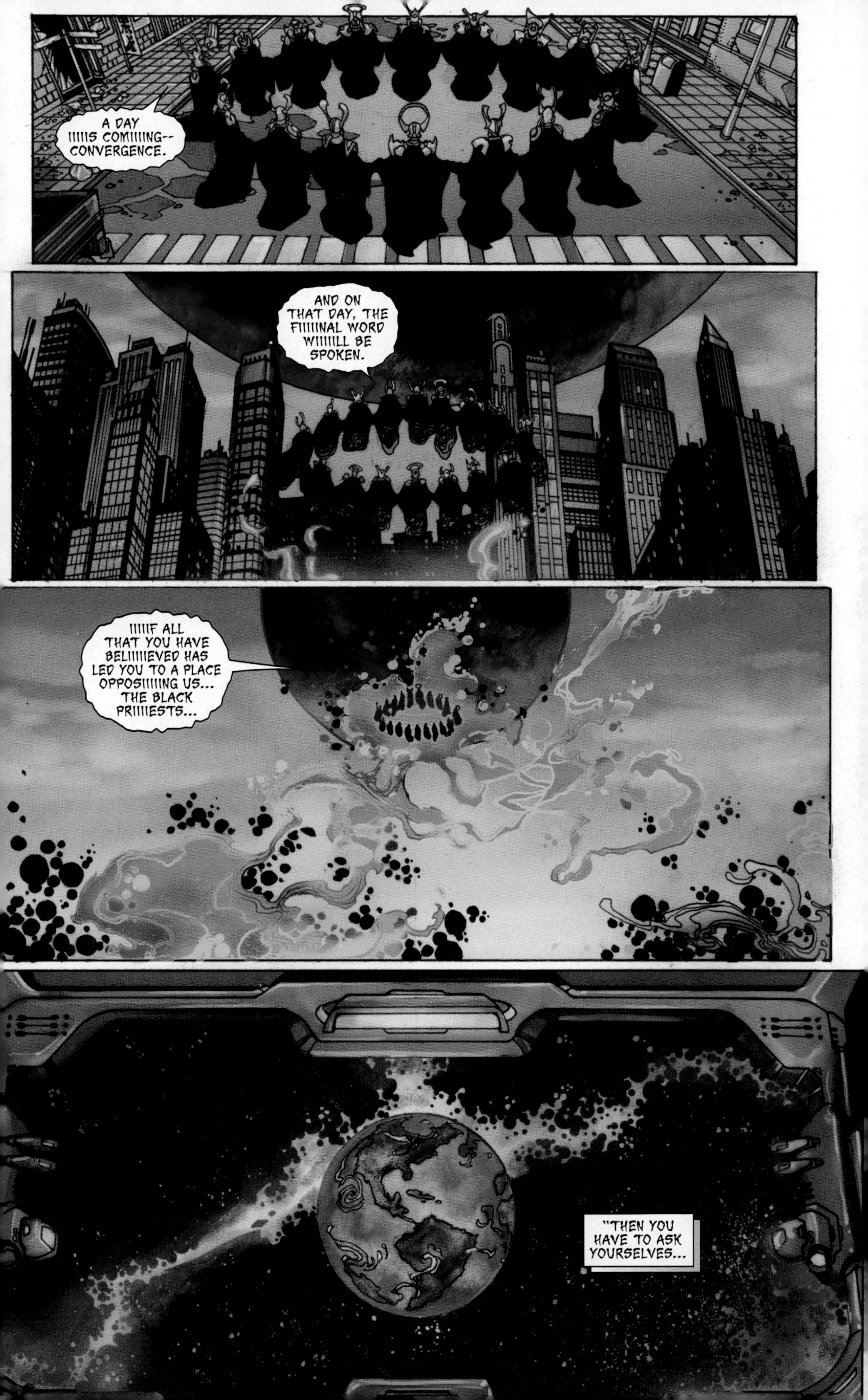
A DAY IIIIIS COMIIIING-- CONVERGENCE.
AND ON THAT DAY, THE FIIIINAL WORD WIIIILL BE SPOKEN.
IIIIIF ALL THAT YOU HAVE BELIIIIEVED HAS LED YOU TO A PLACE OPPOSIIIIING US... THE BLACK PRIIIIESTS...
"THEN YOU HAVE TO ASK YOURSELVES...

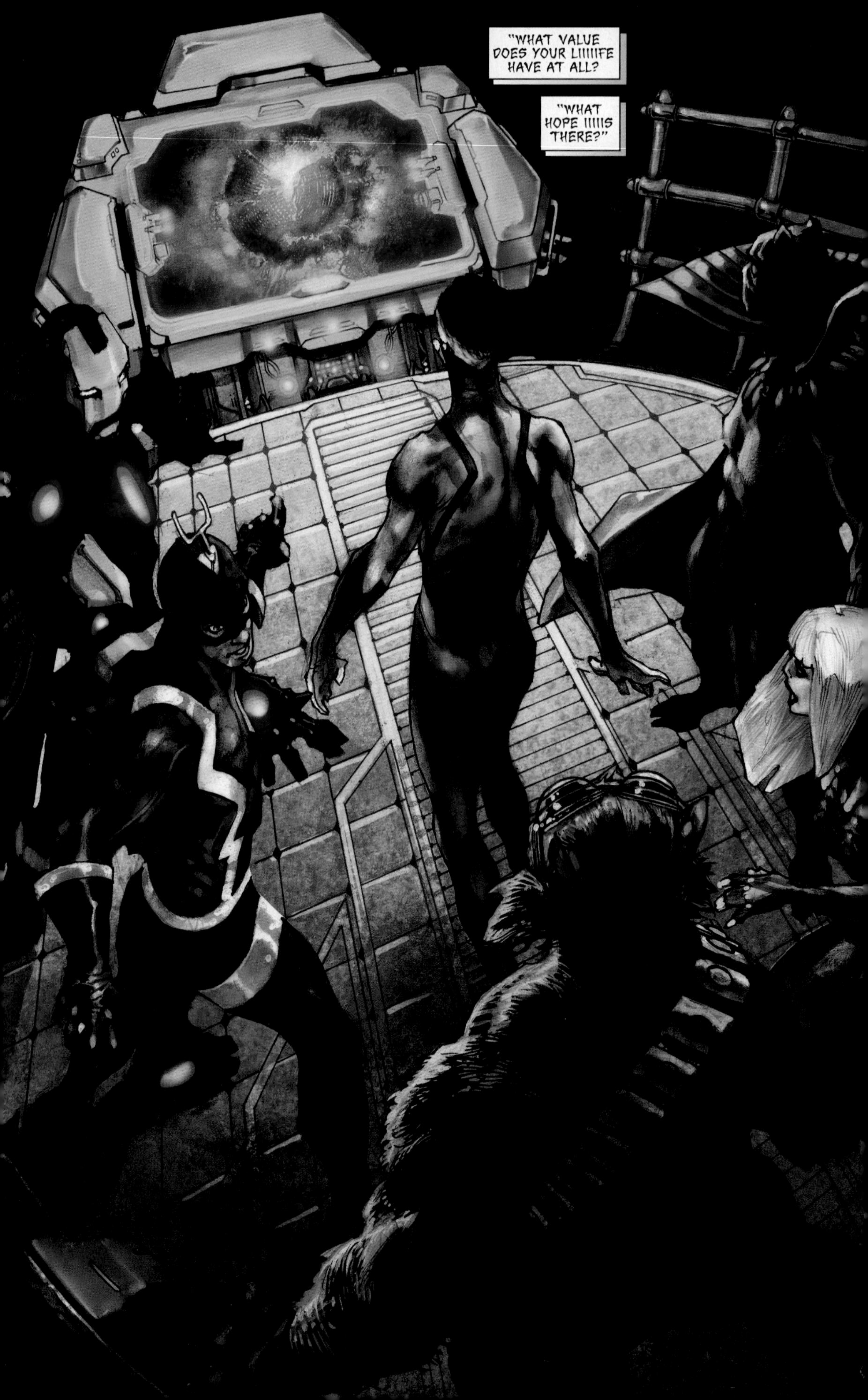
"WHAT VALUE DOES YOUR LIIIIIFE HAVE AT ALL?
"WHAT HOPE IIIIIS THERE?"

"THE AGAMOTTO GAMBIT"

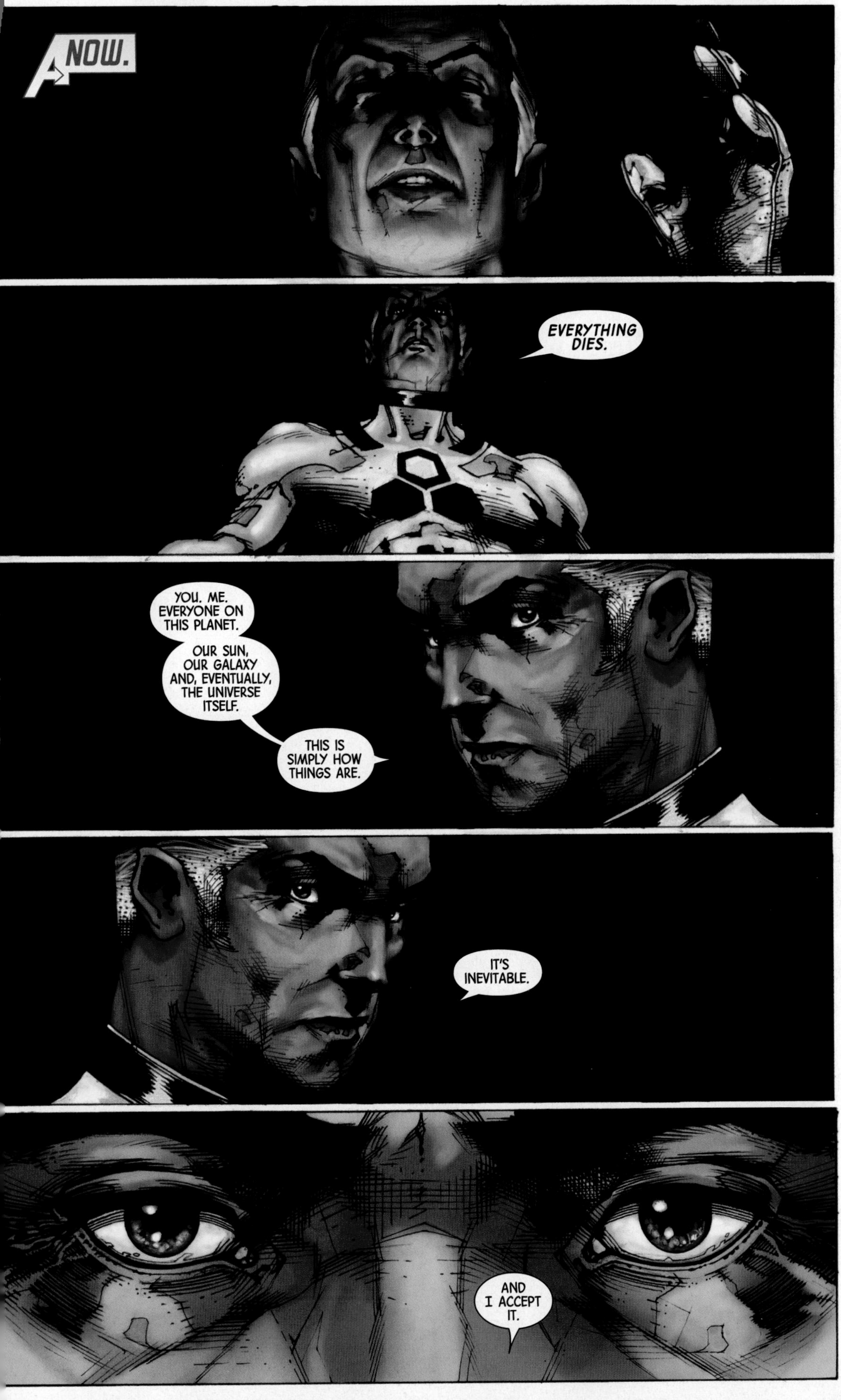
NOW.
EVERYTHING DIES.
YOU. ME. EVERYONE ON THIS PLANET.
OUR SUN, OUR GALAXY AND, EVENTUALLY, THE UNIVERSE ITSELF.
THIS IS SIMPLY HOW THINGS ARE.
IT'S INEVITABLE.
AND I ACCEPT IT.

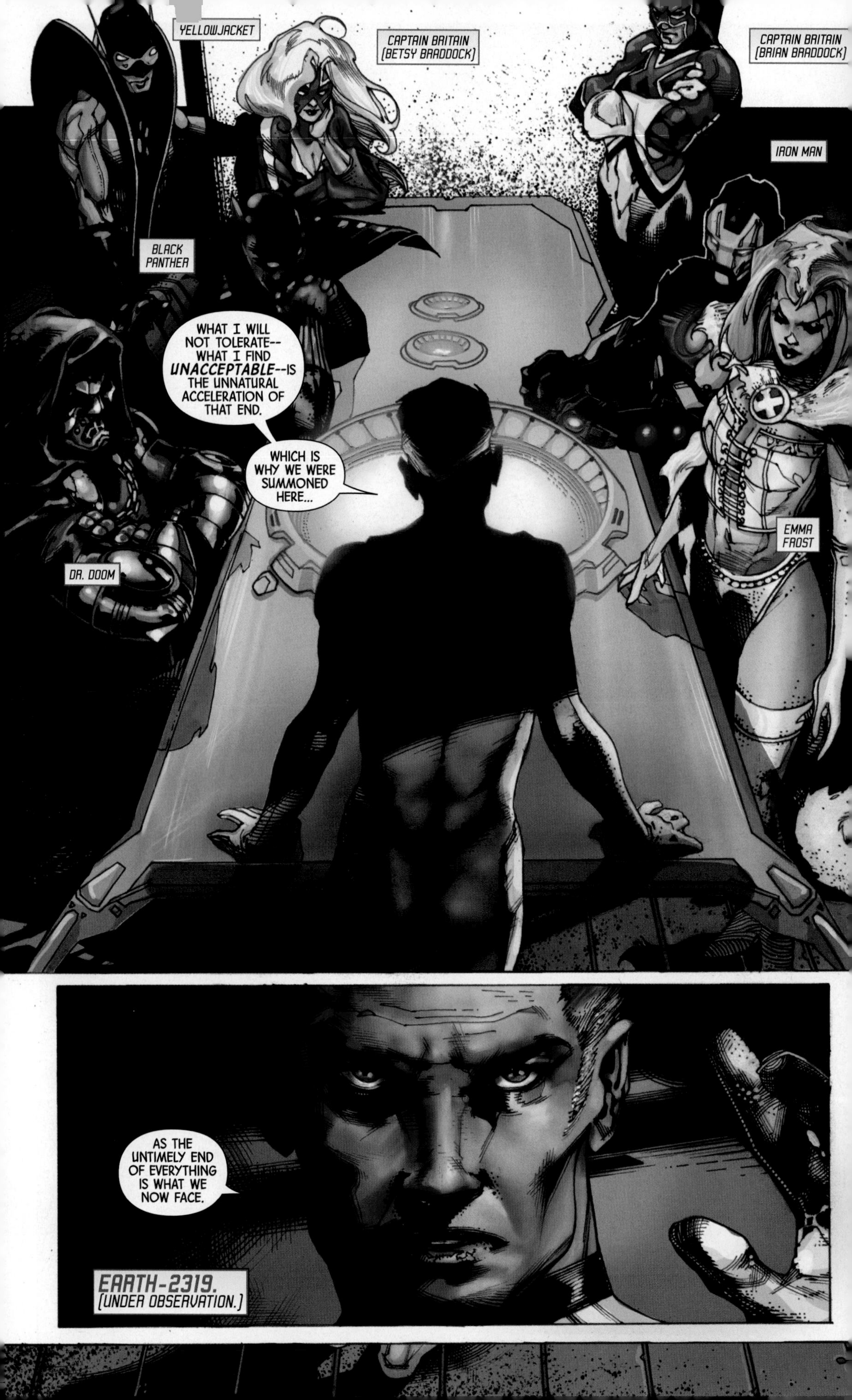
YELLOWJACKET
CAPTAIN BRITAIN (BETSY BRADDOCK)
CAPTAIN BRITAIN (BRIAN BRADDOCK)
IRON MAN
BLACK PANTHER
WHAT I WILL NOT TOLERATE-- WHAT I FIND UNACCEPTABLE--IS THE UNNATURAL ACCELERATION OF THAT END.
WHICH IS WHY WE WERE SUMMONED HERE...
EMMA FROST
DR. DOOM
AS THE UNTIMELY END OF EVERYTHING IS WHAT WE NOW FACE.
EARTH-2319. (UNDER OBSERVATION.)

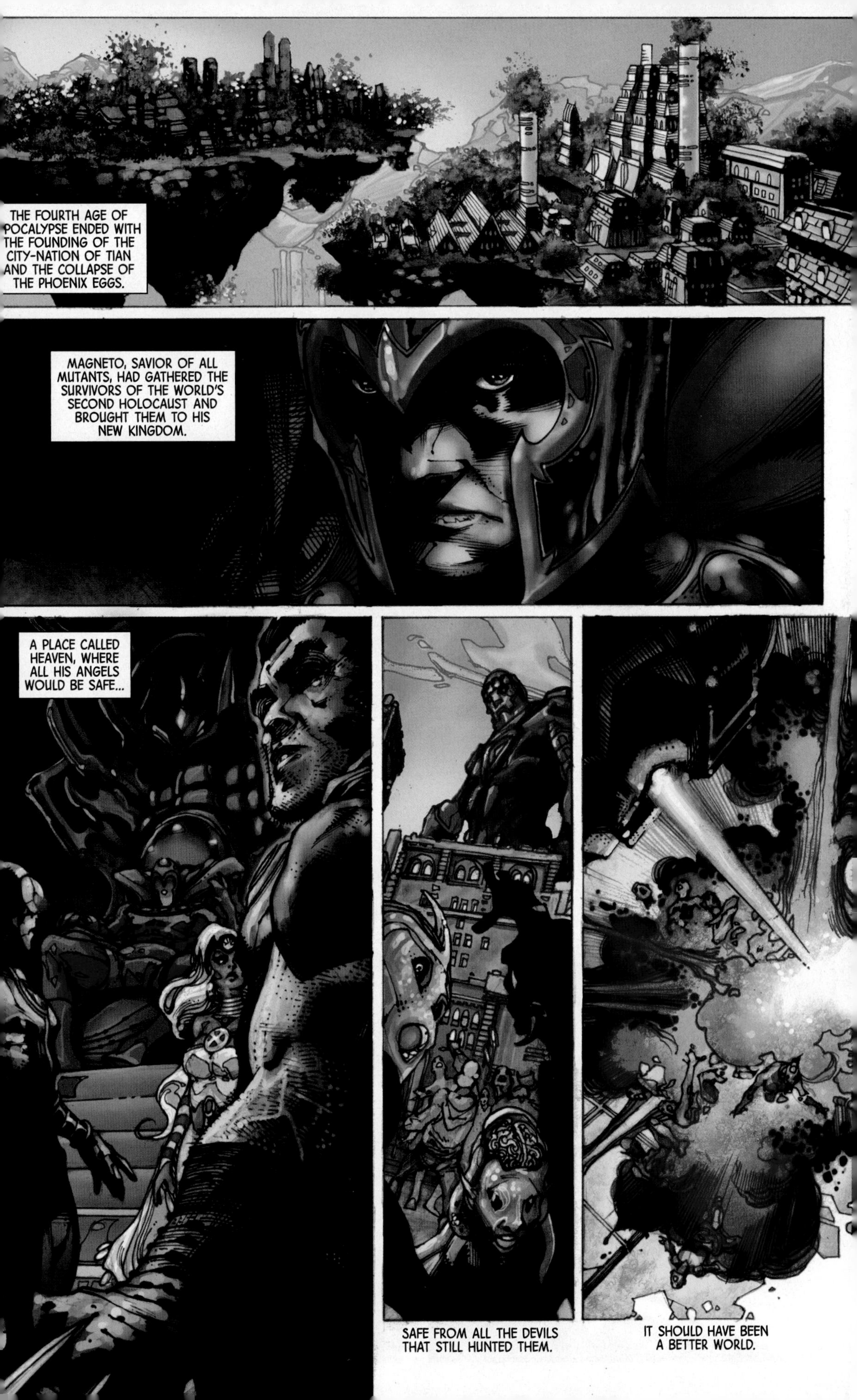
THE FOURTH AGE OF POCALYPSE ENDED WITH THE FOUNDING OF THE CITY-NATION OF TIAN AND THE COLLAPSE OF THE PHOENIX EGGS.
MAGNETO, SAVIOR OF ALL MUTANTS, HAD GATHERED THE SURVIVORS OF THE WORLD'S SECOND HOLOCAUST AND BROUGHT THEM TO HIS NEW KINGDOM.
A PLACE CALLED HEAVEN, WHERE ALL HIS ANGELS WOULD BE SAFE...
SAFE FROM ALL THE DEVILS THAT STILL HUNTED THEM.
IT SHOULD HAVE BEEN A BETTER WORLD.

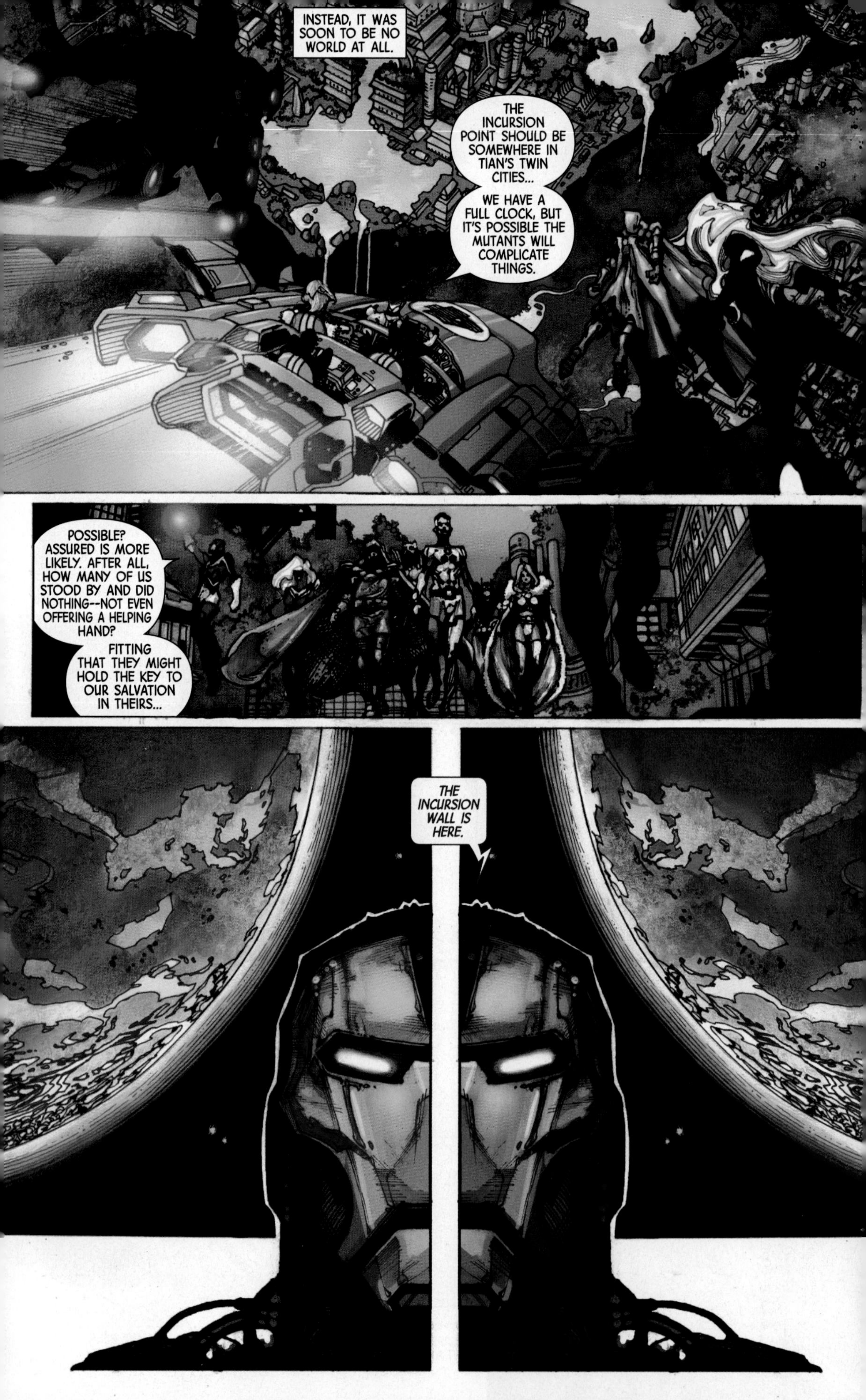
INSTEAD, IT WAS SOON TO BE NO WORLD AT ALL.
THE INCURSION POINT SHOULD BE SOMEWHERE IN TIAN'S TWIN CITIES...
WE HAVE A FULL CLOCK, BUT IT'S POSSIBLE THE MUTANTS WILL COMPLICATE THINGS.
POSSIBLE? ASSURED IS MORE LIKELY. AFTER ALL, HOW MANY OF US STOOD BY AND DID NOTHING--NOT EVEN OFFERING A HELPING HAND?
FITTING THAT THEY MIGHT HOLD THE KEY TO OUR SALVATION IN THEIRS...
THE INCURSION WALL IS HERE.

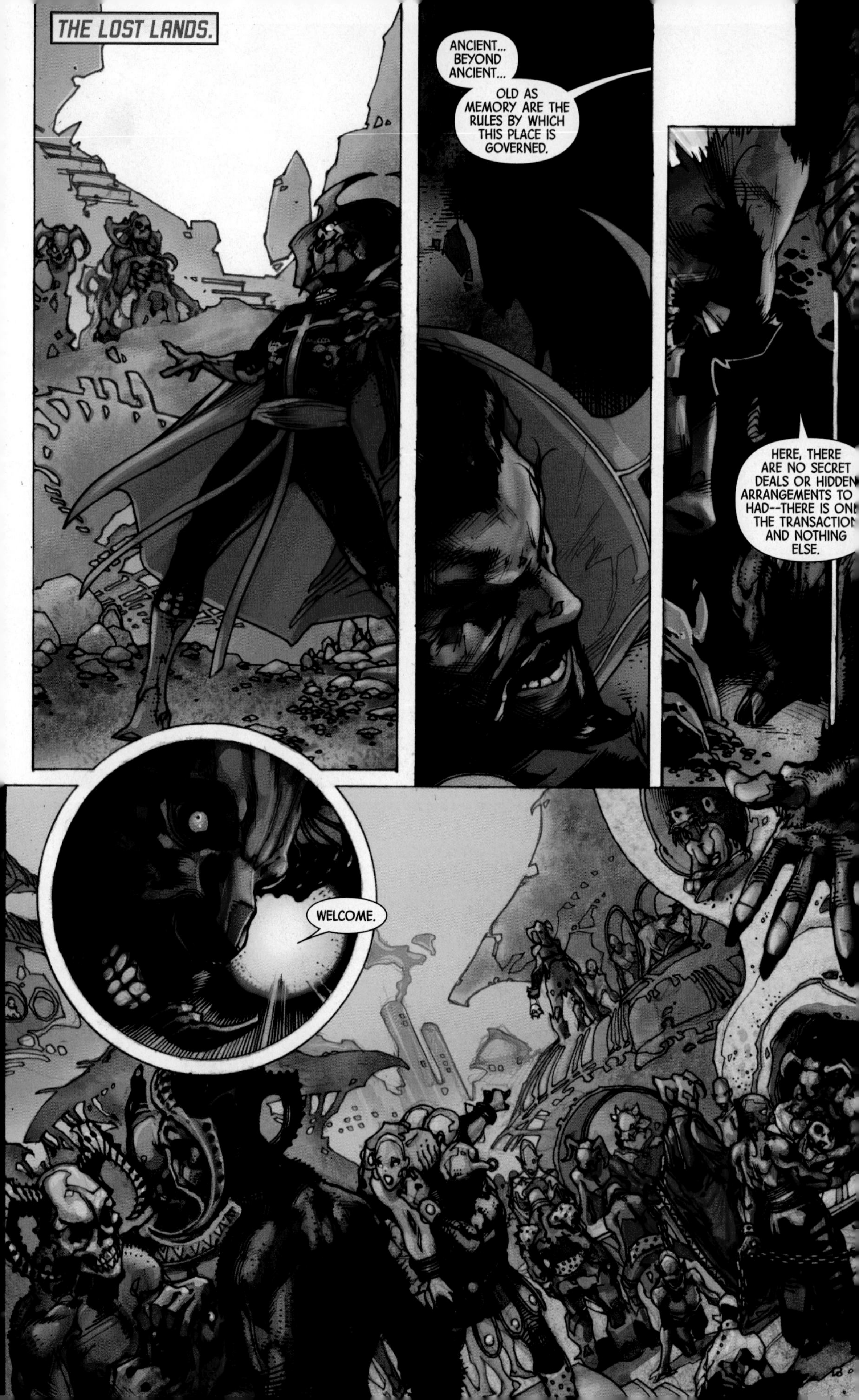
THE LOST LANDS.
ANCIENT... BEYOND ANCIENT...
OLD AS MEMORY ARE THE RULES BY WHICH THIS PLACE IS GOVERNED.
HERE, THERE ARE NO SECRET DEALS OR HIDDEN ARRANGEMENTS TO HAD--THERE IS ON THE TRANSACTIO AND NOTHING ELSE.
WELCOME.

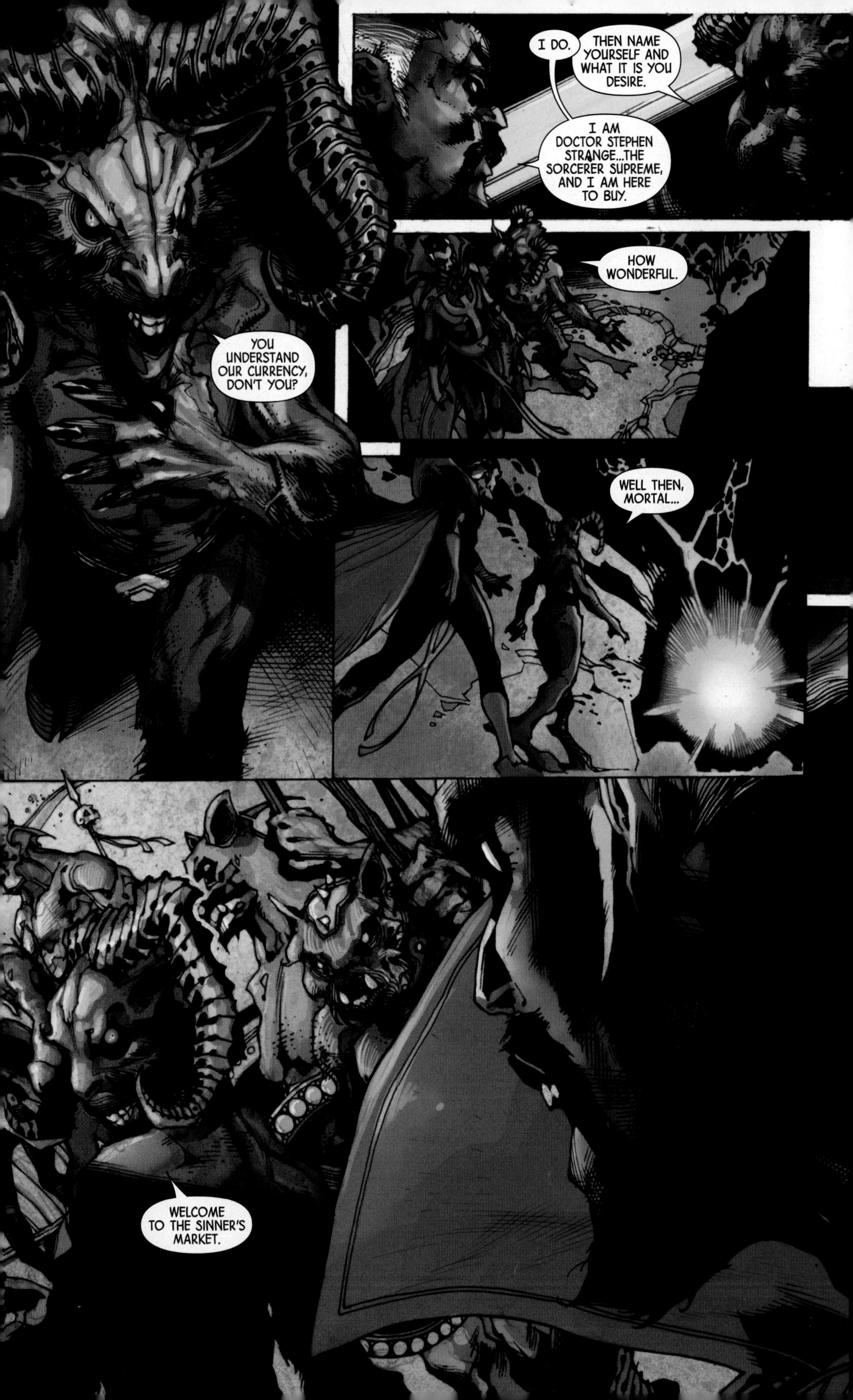
YOU UNDERSTAND OUR CURRENCY, DON'T YOU?
I DO.
THEN NAME YOURSELF AND WHAT IT IS YOU DESIRE.
I AM DOCTOR STEPHEN STRANGE...THE SORCERER SUPREME, AND I AM HERE TO BUY.
HOW WONDERFUL.
WELL THEN, MORTAL...
WELCOME TO THE SINNER'S MARKET.

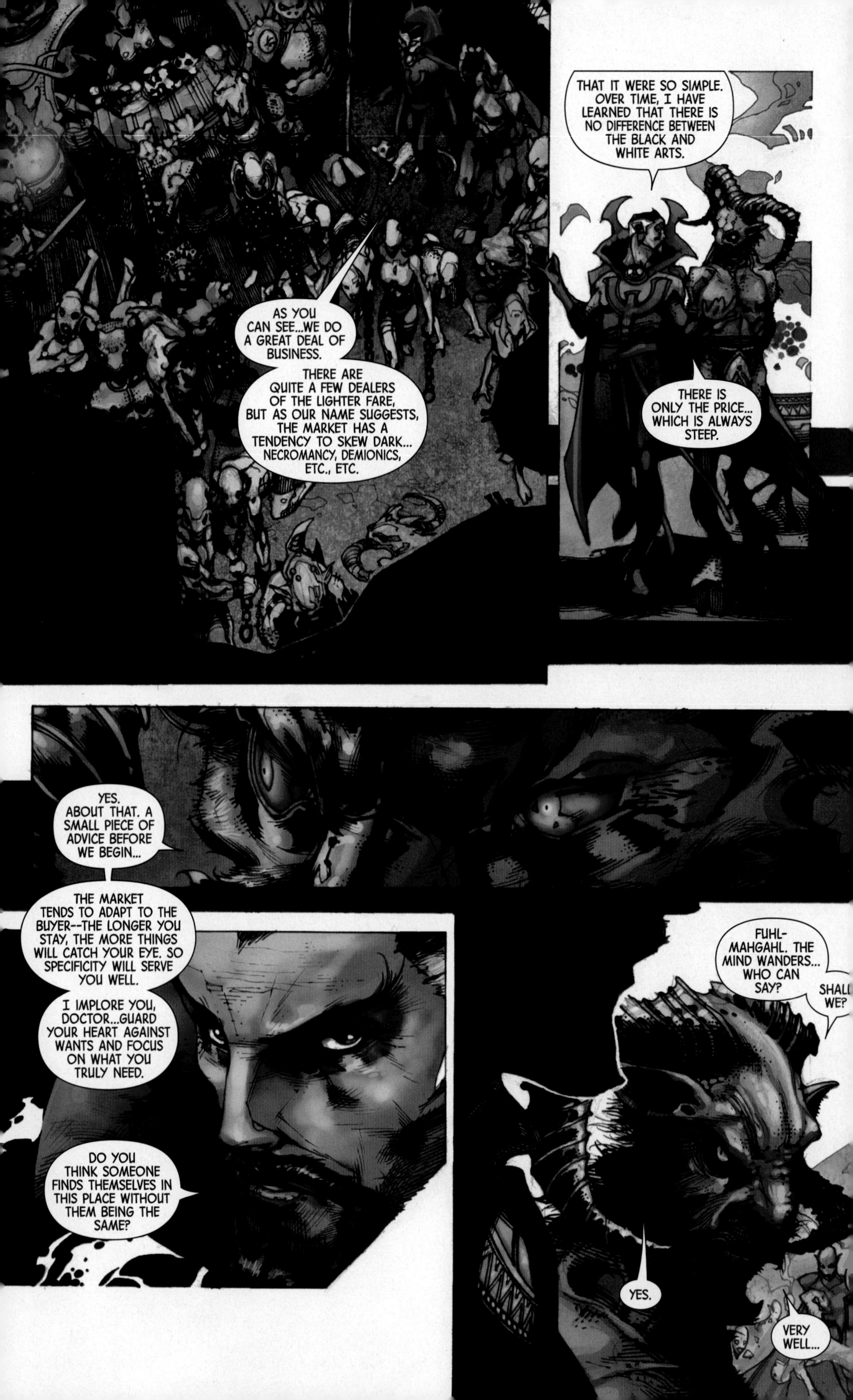
AS YOU CAN SEE...WE DO A GREAT DEAL OF BUSINESS.
THERE ARE QUITE A FEW DEALERS OF THE LIGHTER FARE, BUT AS OUR NAME SUGGESTS, THE MARKET HAS A TENDENCY TO SKEW DARK... NECROMANCY, DEMIONICS, ETC., ETC.
THAT IT WERE SO SIMPLE. OVER TIME, I HAVE LEARNED THAT THERE IS NO DIFFERENCE BETWEEN THE BLACK AND WHITE ARTS.
THERE IS ONLY THE PRICE... WHICH IS ALWAYS STEEP.
YES. ABOUT THAT. A SMALL PIECE OF ADVICE BEFORE WE BEGIN...
THE MARKET TENDS TO ADAPT TO THE BUYER--THE LONGER YOU STAY, THE MORE THINGS WILL CATCH YOUR EYE. SO SPECIFICITY WILL SERVE YOU WELL.
I IMPLORE YOU, DOCTOR...GUARD YOUR HEART AGAINST WANTS AND FOCUS ON WHAT YOU TRULY NEED.
DO YOU THINK SOMEONE FINDS THEMSELVES IN THIS PLACE WITHOUT THEM BEING THE SAME?
FUHL-MAHGAHL. THE MIND WANDERS... WHO CAN SAY?
SHALL WE?
YES.
VERY WELL...

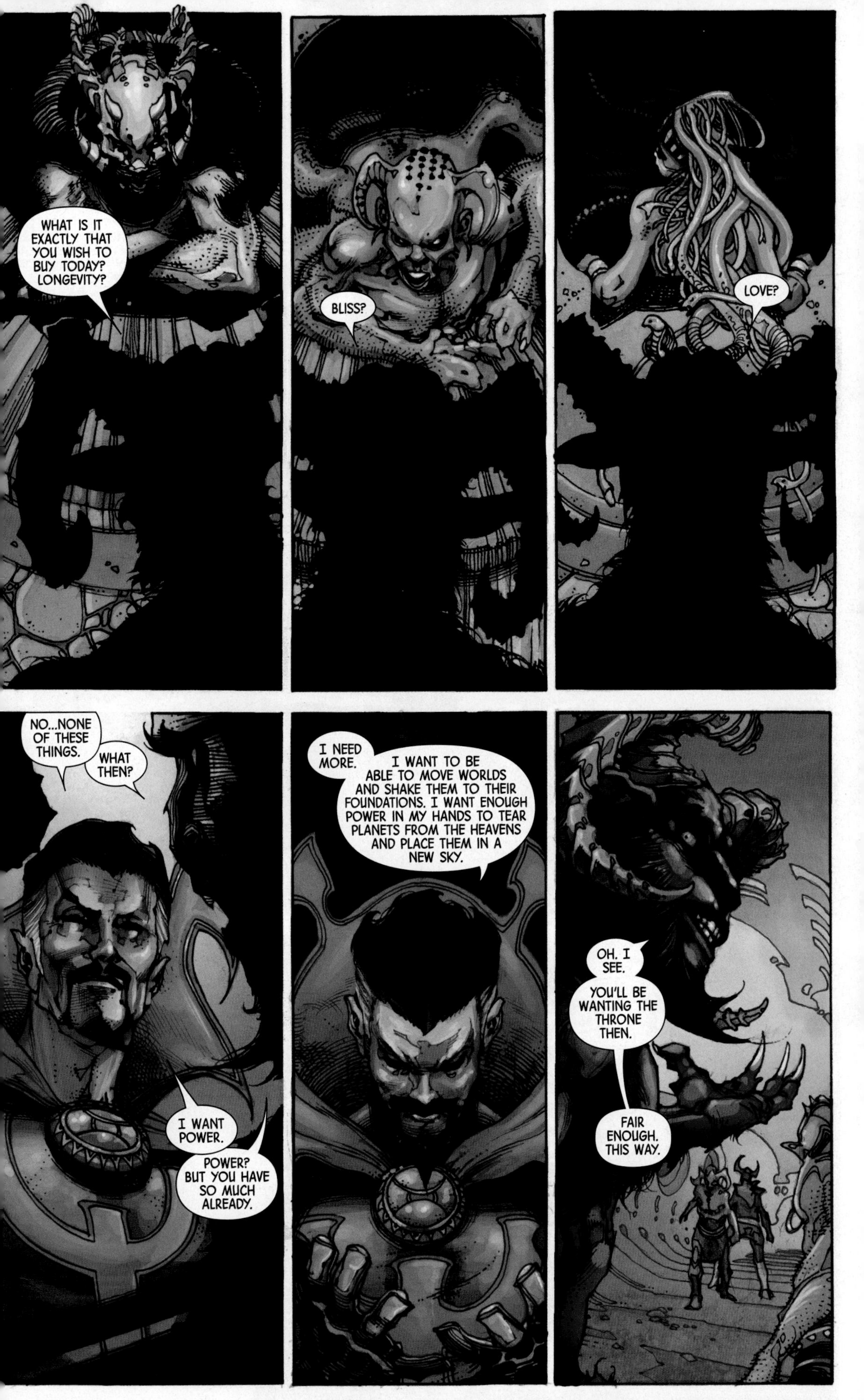
WHAT IS IT EXACTLY THAT YOU WISH TO BUY TODAY? LONGEVITY?
BLISS?
LOVE?
NO...NONE OF THESE THINGS.
WHAT THEN?
I WANT POWER.
POWER? BUT YOU HAVE SO MUCH ALREADY.
I NEED MORE.
I WANT TO BE ABLE TO MOVE WORLDS AND SHAKE THEM TO THEIR FOUNDATIONS. I WANT ENOUGH POWER IN MY HANDS TO TEAR PLANETS FROM THE HEAVENS AND PLACE THEM IN A NEW SKY.
OH. I SEE.
YOU'LL BE WANTING THE THRONE THEN.
FAIR ENOUGH. THIS WAY.

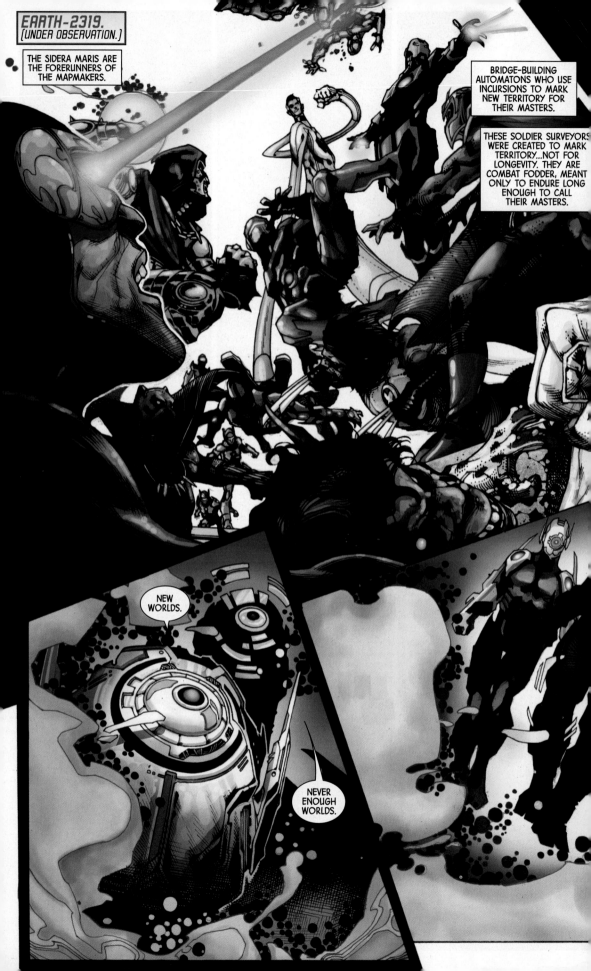

EARTH-2319.
[UNDER OBSERVATION.]

THE SIDERA MARIS ARE THE FORERUNNERS OF THE MAPMAKERS.

BRIDGE-BUILDING AUTOMATONS WHO USE INCURSIONS TO MARK NEW TERRITORY FOR THEIR MASTERS.

THESE SOLDIER SURVEYORS WERE CREATED TO MARK TERRITORY...NOT FOR LONGEVITY. THEY ARE COMBAT FODDER, MEANT ONLY TO ENDURE LONG ENOUGH TO CALL THEIR MASTERS.

NEW WORLDS.

NEVER ENOUGH WORLDS.

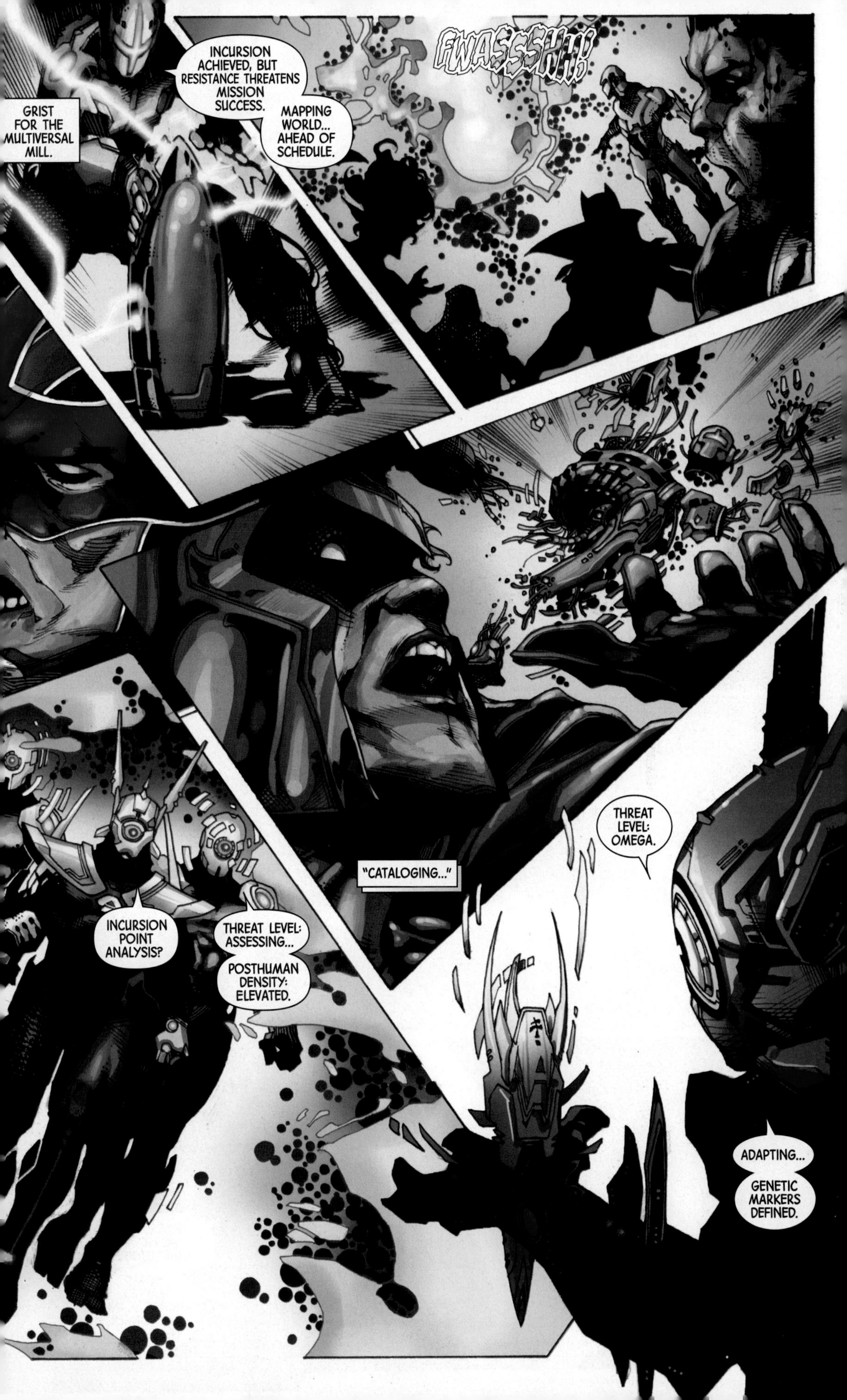
GRIST FOR THE MULTIVERSAL MILL.
INCURSION ACHIEVED, BUT RESISTANCE THREATENS MISSION SUCCESS.
MAPPING WORLD... AHEAD OF SCHEDULE.
FWASSSHH!
"CATALOGING..."
THREAT LEVEL: OMEGA.
INCURSION POINT ANALYSIS?
THREAT LEVEL: ASSESSING...
POSTHUMAN DENSITY: ELEVATED.
ADAPTING...
GENETIC MARKERS DEFINED.

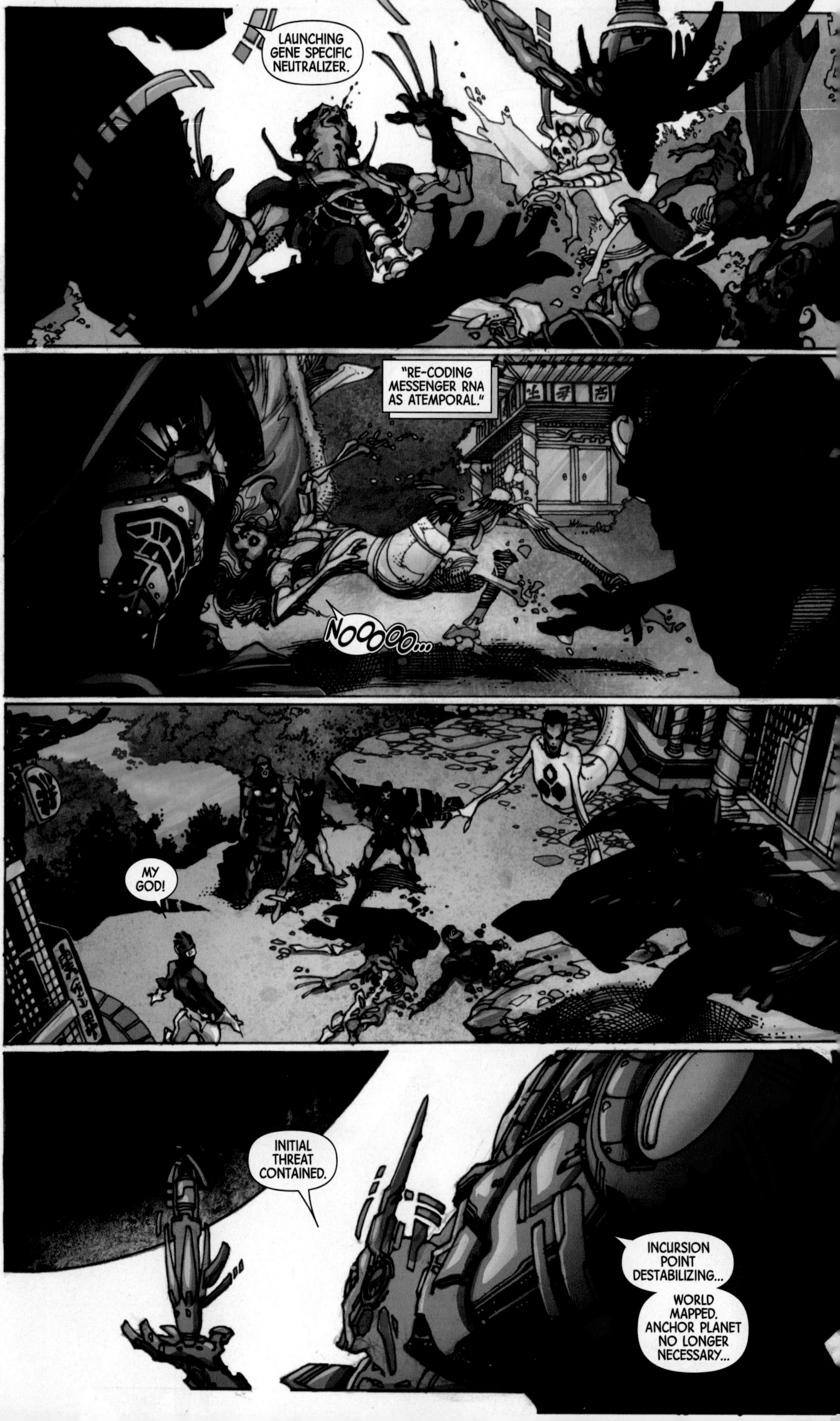
LAUNCHING GENE SPECIFIC NEUTRALIZER.
"RE-CODING MESSENGER RNA AS ATEMPORAL."
NOOOOO...
MY GOD!
INITIAL THREAT CONTAINED.
INCURSION POINT DESTABILIZING...
WORLD MAPPED. ANCHOR PLANET NO LONGER NECESSARY...

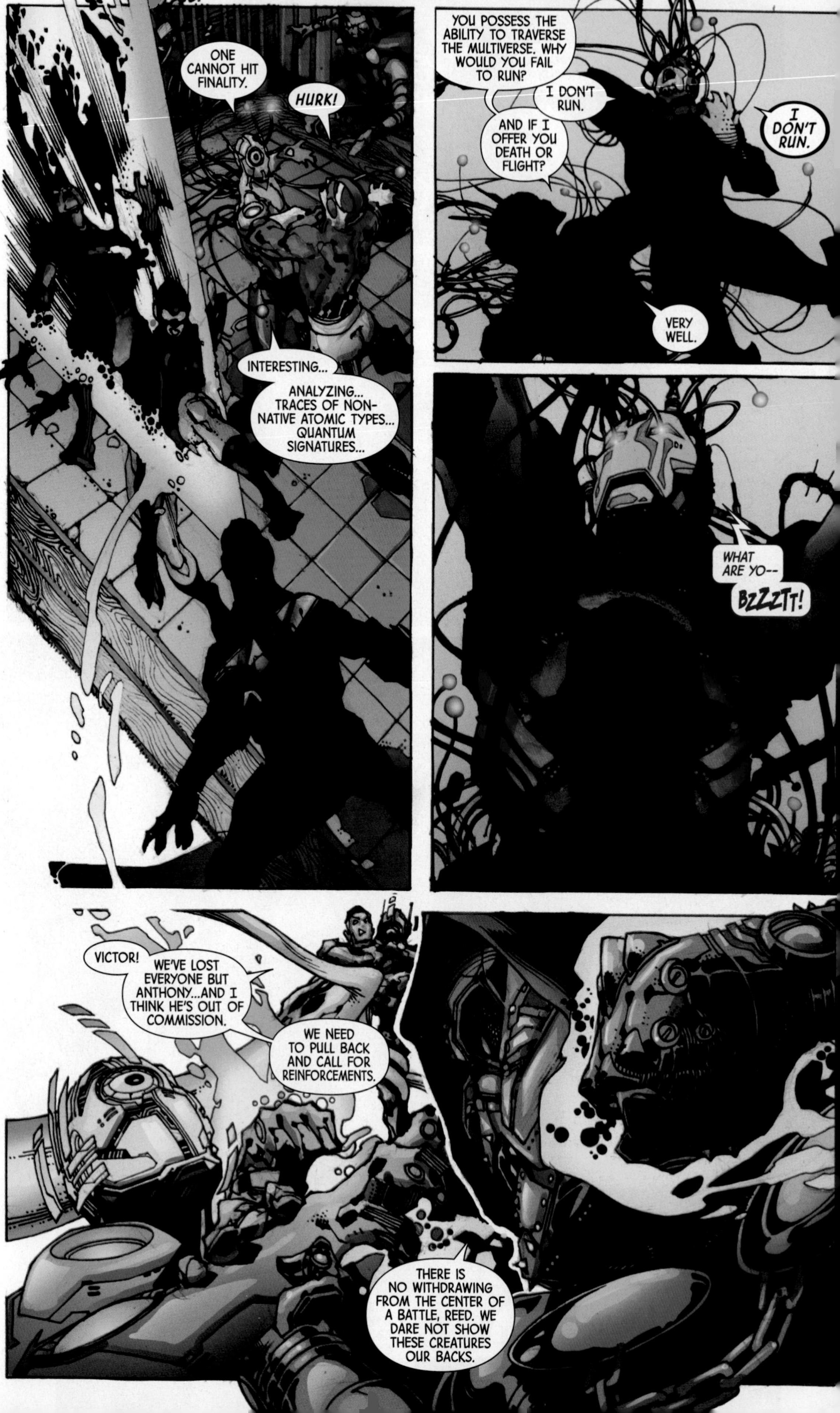

ONE CANNOT HIT FINALITY.
HURK!
INTERESTING...
ANALYZING... TRACES OF NON-NATIVE ATOMIC TYPES... QUANTUM SIGNATURES...
YOU POSSESS THE ABILITY TO TRAVERSE THE MULTIVERSE. WHY WOULD YOU FAIL TO RUN?
I DON'T RUN.
AND IF I OFFER YOU DEATH OR FLIGHT?
I DON'T RUN.
VERY WELL.
WHAT ARE YO--
BZZZTT!
VICTOR!
WE'VE LOST EVERYONE BUT ANTHONY...AND I THINK HE'S OUT OF COMMISSION.
WE NEED TO PULL BACK AND CALL FOR REINFORCEMENTS.
THERE IS NO WITHDRAWING FROM THE CENTER OF A BATTLE, REED. WE DARE NOT SHOW THESE CREATURES OUR BACKS.

BESIDES...

WHY FLEE FROM THAT WHICH CAN BE CONQUERED?

OMEGA-LEVEL THREAT DETECTED.

THAT MAKER ACHIEVED CONSCIOUSNESS ONE HUNDRED CYCLES AGO. IT MAPPED THOUSANDS OF EARTHS.

IT WAS... IRREPLACEABLE.

PRIORITY OVERRIDE.

LOSS OF FULL HARVEST... ACCEPTABLE.

VICTOR! LOOK OUT!

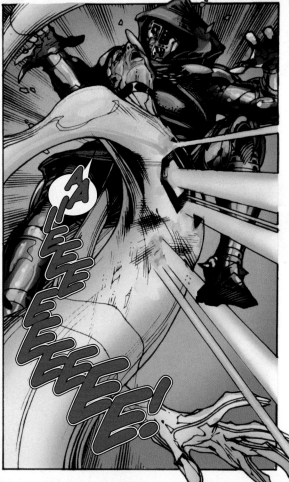

AIEEEEEEEEEEE!

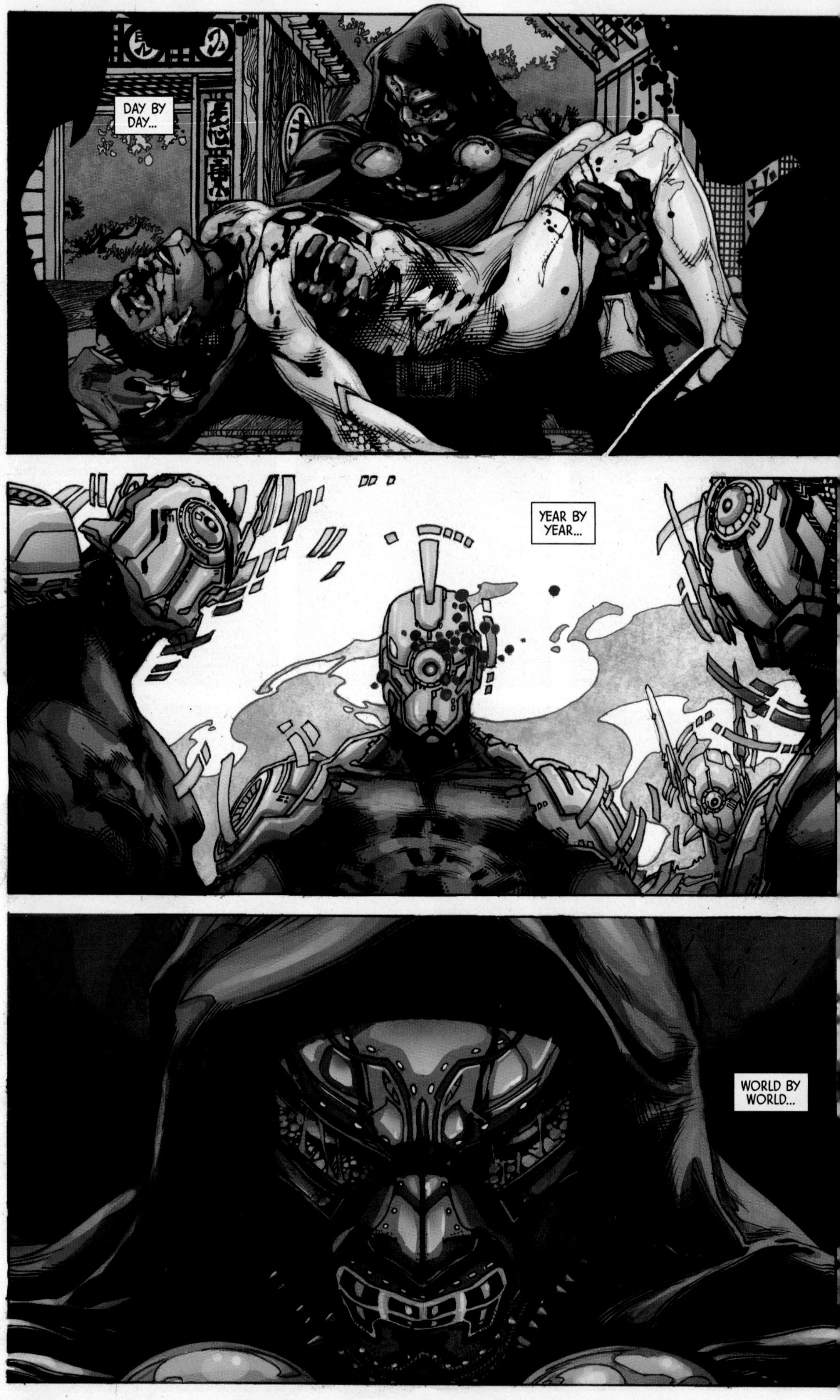
DAY BY DAY...
YEAR BY YEAR...
WORLD BY WORLD...

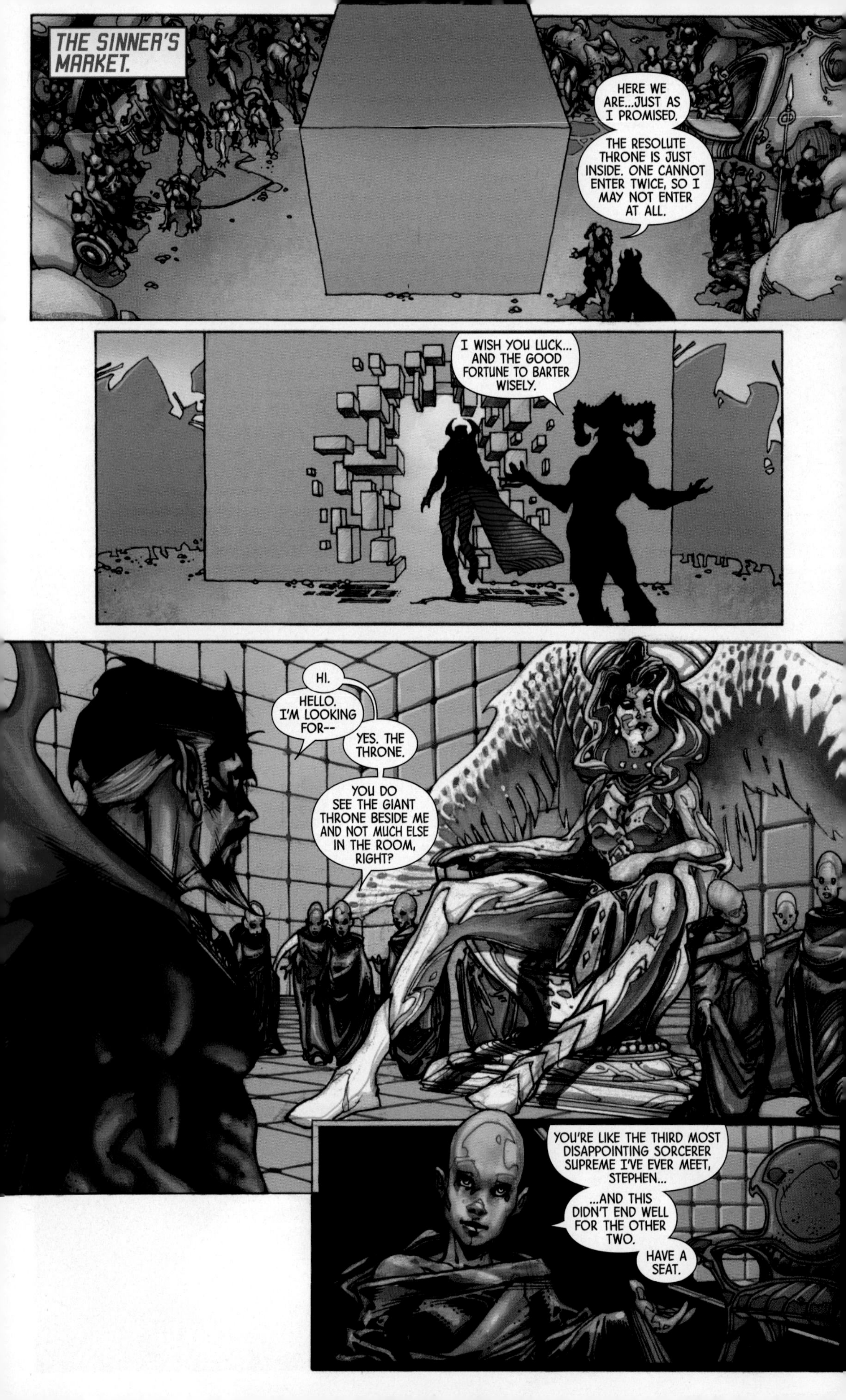
THE SINNER'S MARKET.
HERE WE ARE...JUST AS I PROMISED.
THE RESOLUTE THRONE IS JUST INSIDE. ONE CANNOT ENTER TWICE, SO I MAY NOT ENTER AT ALL.
I WISH YOU LUCK... AND THE GOOD FORTUNE TO BARTER WISELY.
HI.
HELLO. I'M LOOKING FOR--
YES. THE THRONE.
YOU DO SEE THE GIANT THRONE BESIDE ME AND NOT MUCH ELSE IN THE ROOM, RIGHT?
YOU'RE LIKE THE THIRD MOST DISAPPOINTING SORCERER SUPREME I'VE EVER MEET, STEPHEN...
...AND THIS DIDN'T END WELL FOR THE OTHER TWO.
HAVE A SEAT.

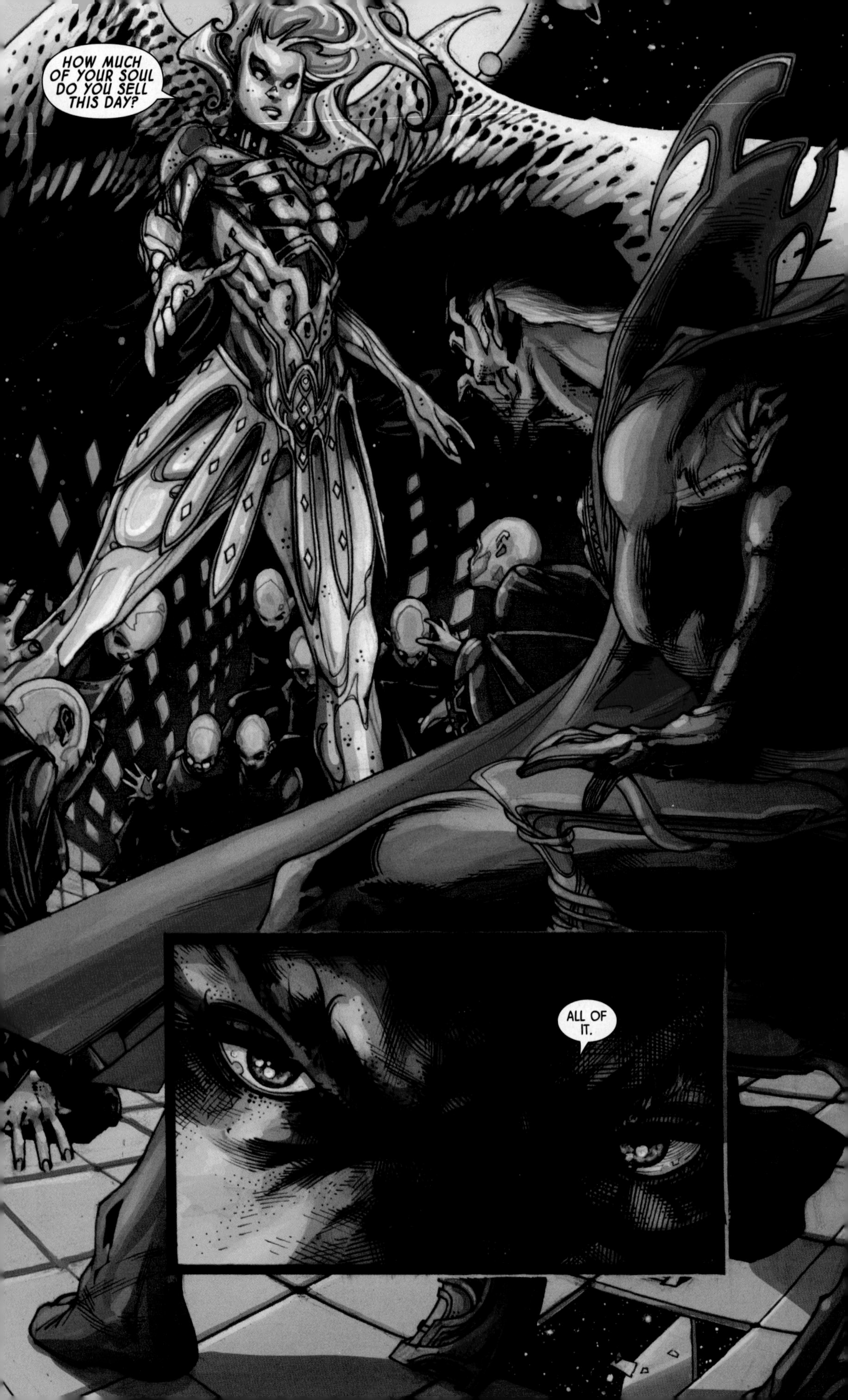
HOW MUCH OF YOUR SOUL DO YOU SELL THIS DAY?
ALL OF IT.

"SEE HOW THE SWANS FLY"

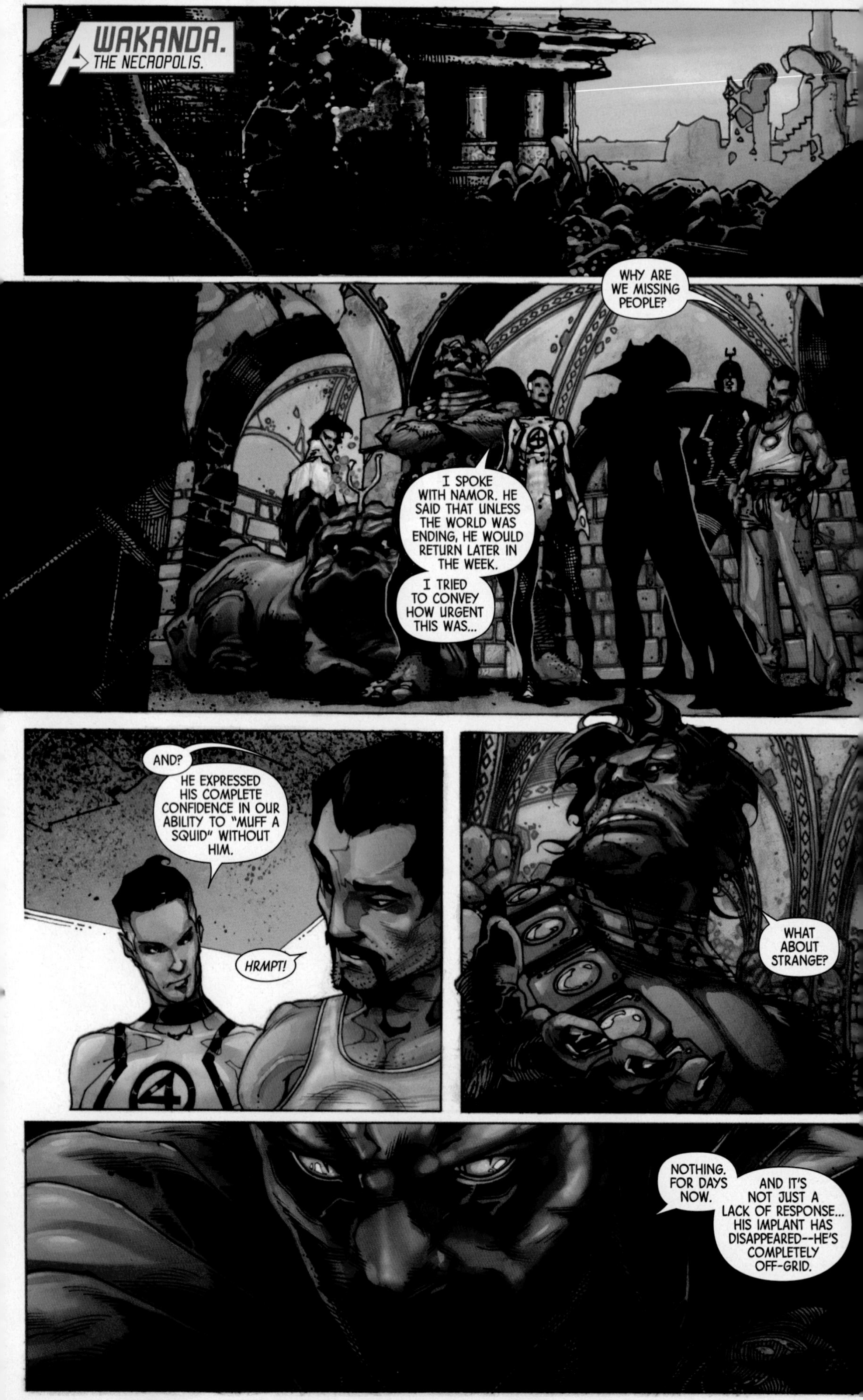

WAKANDA.
THE NECROPOLIS.
WHY ARE WE MISSING PEOPLE?
I SPOKE WITH NAMOR. HE SAID THAT UNLESS THE WORLD WAS ENDING, HE WOULD RETURN LATER IN THE WEEK.
I TRIED TO CONVEY HOW URGENT THIS WAS...
AND?
HE EXPRESSED HIS COMPLETE CONFIDENCE IN OUR ABILITY TO "MUFF A SQUID" WITHOUT HIM.
HRMPT!
WHAT ABOUT STRANGE?
NOTHING. FOR DAYS NOW.
AND IT'S NOT JUST A LACK OF RESPONSE... HIS IMPLANT HAS DISAPPEARED--HE'S COMPLETELY OFF-GRID.

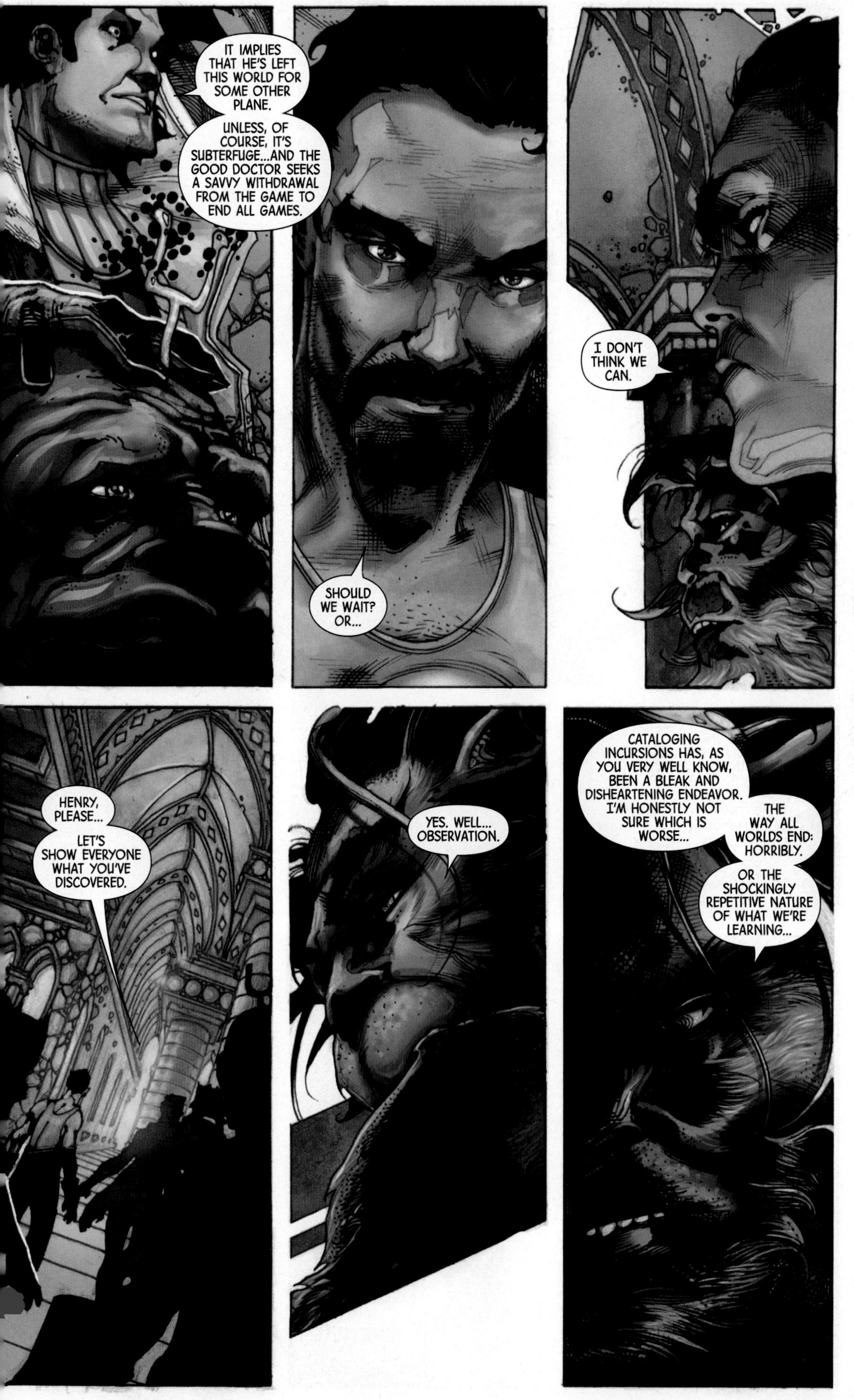
IT IMPLIES THAT HE'S LEFT THIS WORLD FOR SOME OTHER PLANE.
UNLESS, OF COURSE, IT'S SUBTERFUGE...AND THE GOOD DOCTOR SEEKS A SAVVY WITHDRAWAL FROM THE GAME TO END ALL GAMES.
SHOULD WE WAIT? OR...
I DON'T THINK WE CAN.
HENRY, PLEASE...
LET'S SHOW EVERYONE WHAT YOU'VE DISCOVERED.
YES. WELL... OBSERVATION.
CATALOGING INCURSIONS HAS, AS YOU VERY WELL KNOW, BEEN A BLEAK AND DISHEARTENING ENDEAVOR. I'M HONESTLY NOT SURE WHICH IS WORSE...
THE WAY ALL WORLDS END: HORRIBLY.
OR THE SHOCKINGLY REPETITIVE NATURE OF WHAT WE'RE LEARNING...

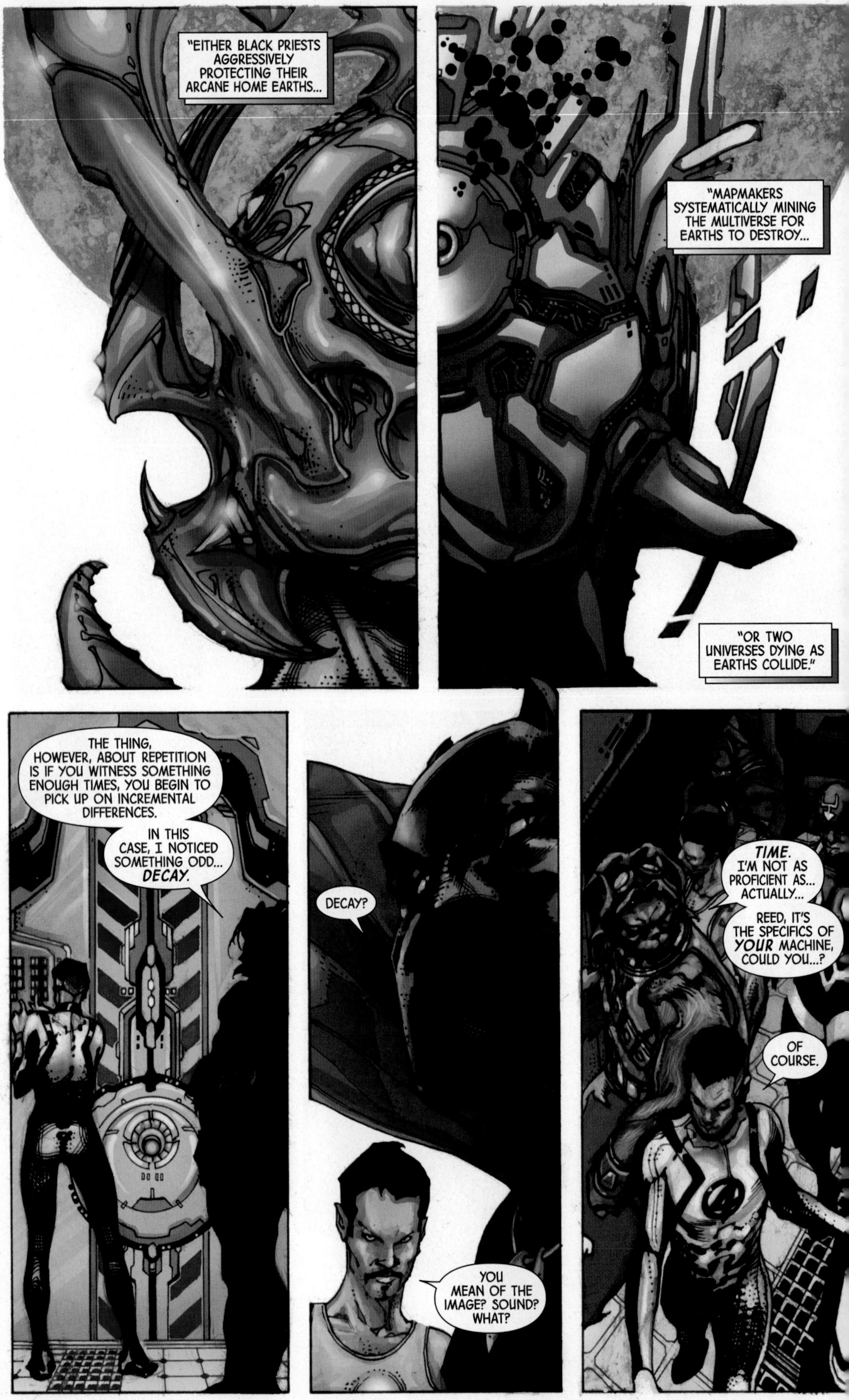
"EITHER BLACK PRIESTS AGGRESSIVELY PROTECTING THEIR ARCANE HOME EARTHS...
"MAPMAKERS SYSTEMATICALLY MINING THE MULTIVERSE FOR EARTHS TO DESTROY...
"OR TWO UNIVERSES DYING AS EARTHS COLLIDE."
THE THING, HOWEVER, ABOUT REPETITION IS IF YOU WITNESS SOMETHING ENOUGH TIMES, YOU BEGIN TO PICK UP ON INCREMENTAL DIFFERENCES.
IN THIS CASE, I NOTICED SOMETHING ODD... DECAY.
DECAY?
YOU MEAN OF THE IMAGE? SOUND? WHAT?
TIME. I'M NOT AS PROFICIENT AS... ACTUALLY...
REED, IT'S THE SPECIFICS OF YOUR MACHINE, COULD YOU...?
OF COURSE.

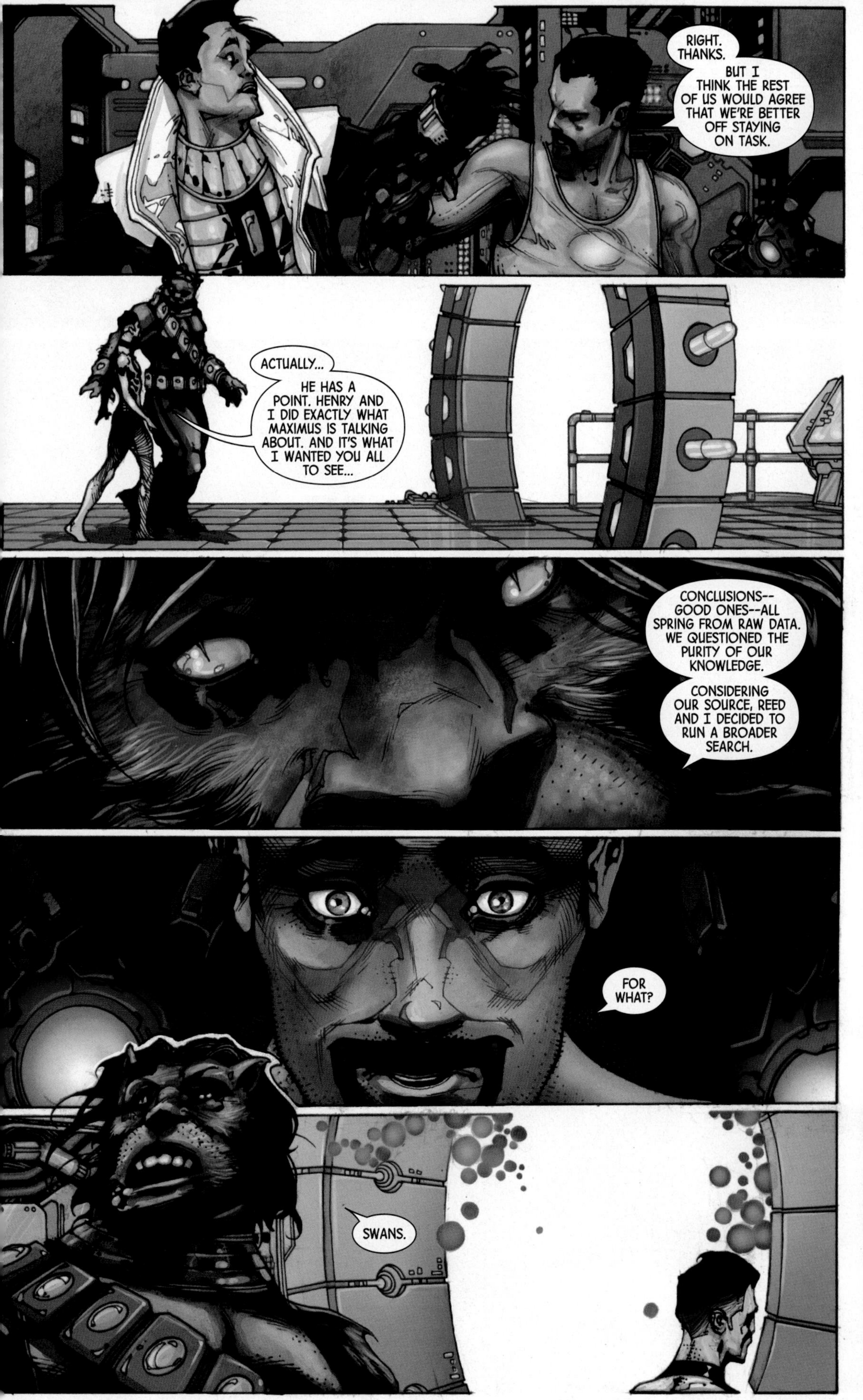
RIGHT. THANKS.
BUT I THINK THE REST OF US WOULD AGREE THAT WE'RE BETTER OFF STAYING ON TASK.
ACTUALLY...
HE HAS A POINT. HENRY AND I DID EXACTLY WHAT MAXIMUS IS TALKING ABOUT. AND IT'S WHAT I WANTED YOU ALL TO SEE...
CONCLUSIONS-- GOOD ONES--ALL SPRING FROM RAW DATA. WE QUESTIONED THE PURITY OF OUR KNOWLEDGE.
CONSIDERING OUR SOURCE, REED AND I DECIDED TO RUN A BROADER SEARCH.
FOR WHAT?
SWANS.

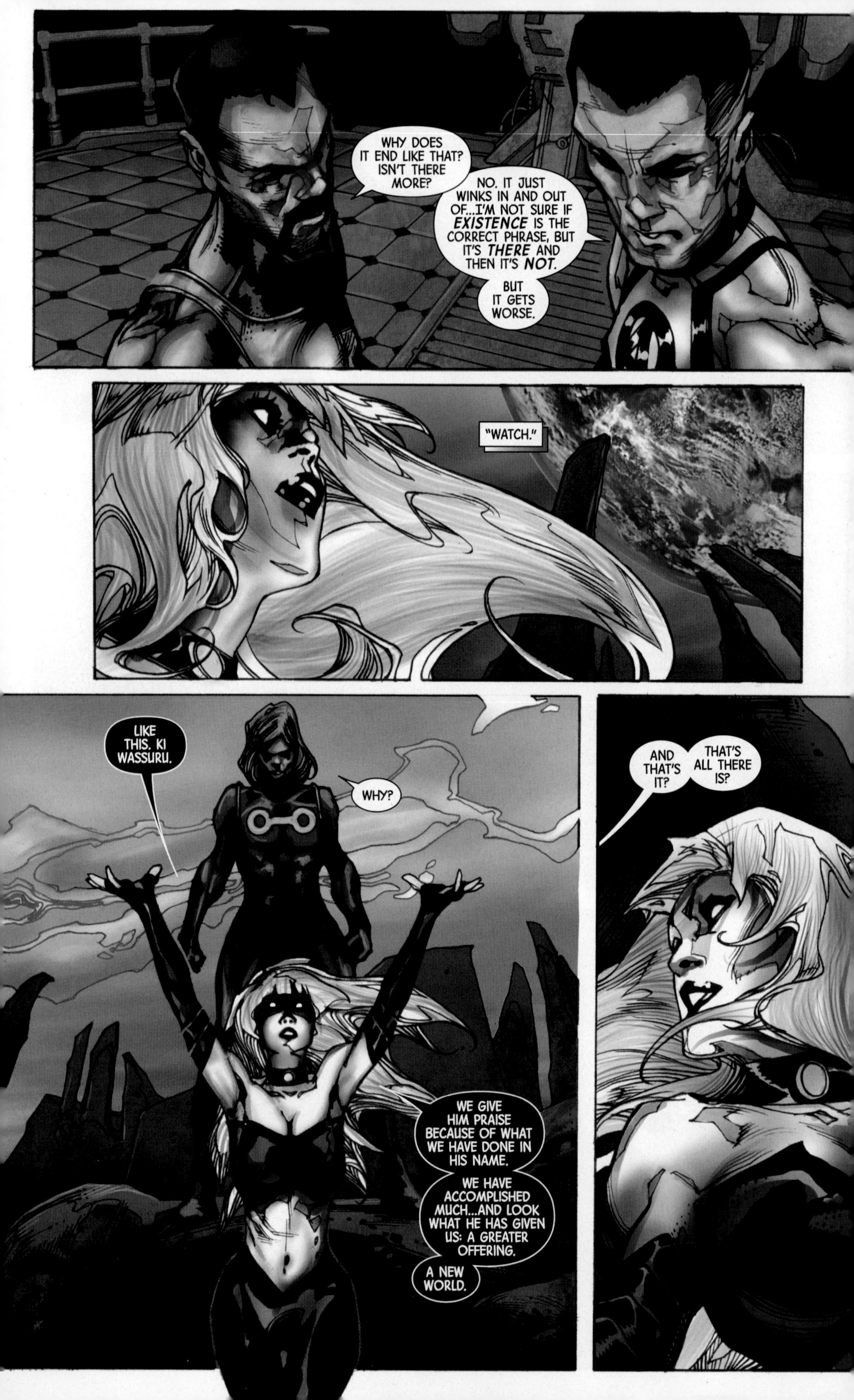
WHY DOES IT END LIKE THAT? ISN'T THERE MORE?
NO. IT JUST WINKS IN AND OUT OF...I'M NOT SURE IF *EXISTENCE* IS THE CORRECT PHRASE, BUT IT'S *THERE* AND THEN IT'S *NOT*.
BUT IT GETS WORSE.
"WATCH."
LIKE THIS, KI WASSURU.
WHY?
WE GIVE HIM PRAISE BECAUSE OF WHAT WE HAVE DONE IN HIS NAME.
WE HAVE ACCOMPLISHED MUCH...AND LOOK WHAT HE HAS GIVEN US: A GREATER OFFERING.
A NEW WORLD.
AND THAT'S IT?
THAT'S ALL THERE IS?

BUT I HAVE FOUND THAT...**THIS EXISTENCE** PROVIDES M THE SOLITUDE NECESSAR TO TRULY CONTEMPLATE OUR PLACE IN THESE...TH LAST GASPS OF A DYING MULTIVERSE.

I WILL NOT TELL YOU THAT YOU WON'T MISS YOUR FREEDOM.

YOU WILL.

ARE YOU TELLING ME TO BE THANKFUL?

THIS IS THE WISDOM OF TERRAX THE ENLIGHTENED?

I'M SAYING THAT IN HERE IT SEEMS EVERYTHING STAYS THE SAME, WHILE **OUT THERE** EVERYTHING CONTINUES TO DIE.

I BELIEVE IN THE WHEEL--I DO NOT SEEK LIFE, HERALD.

I AM NOT LOOKING TO SAVE MYSELF OR AVOID MY FATE!

LIFE. DEATH. WHAT'S THE DIFFERENCE? TIME? WHAT FOOL SEES **THAT** AS A CONSTANT?

IT'S ALL YOUR WHEEL, ISN'T IT? DO THE TWO NOT BECOME THE SAME?

YOU HAVE A POINT TO MAKE?

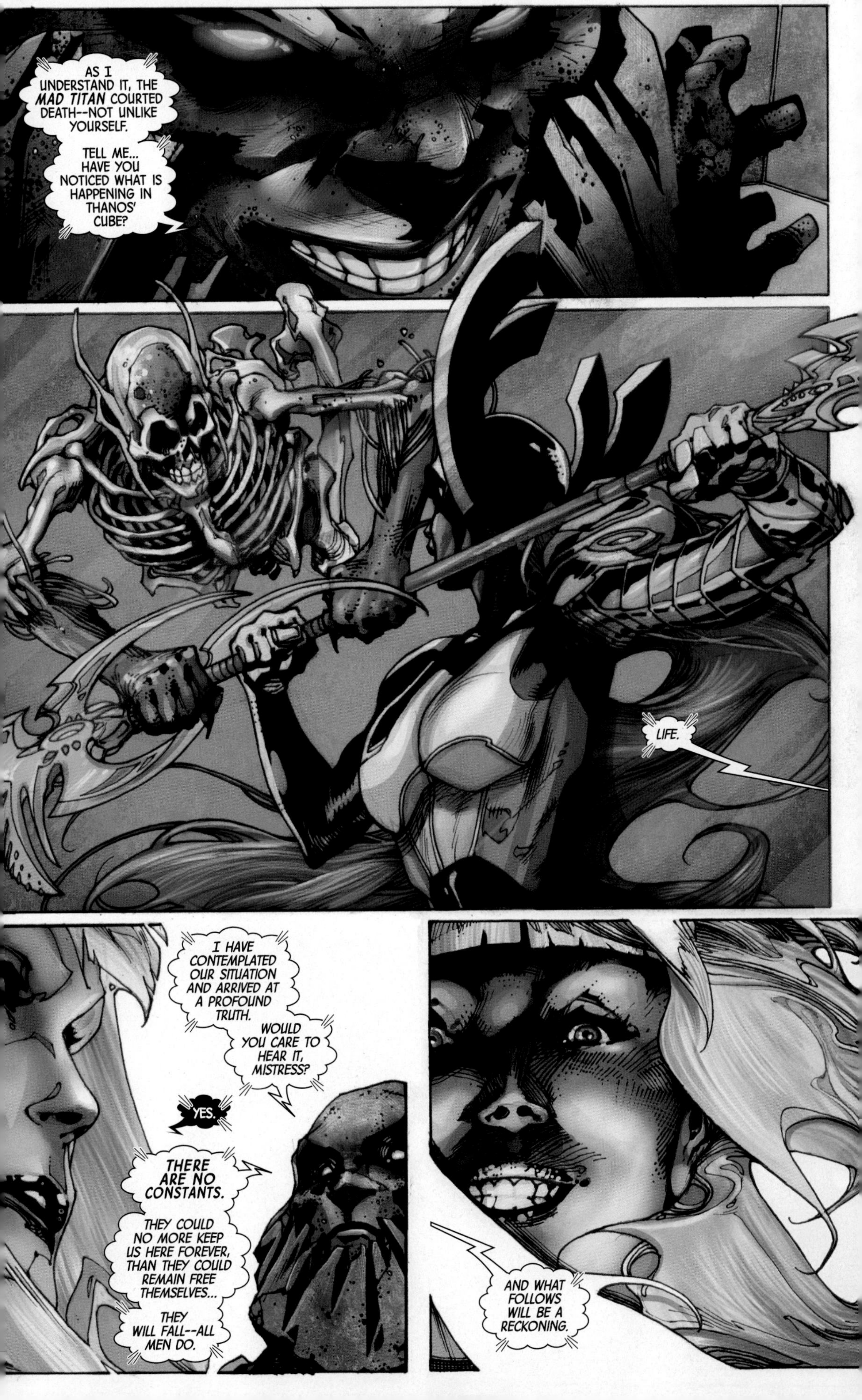
AS I UNDERSTAND IT, THE MAD TITAN COURTED DEATH--NOT UNLIKE YOURSELF.
TELL ME... HAVE YOU NOTICED WHAT IS HAPPENING IN THANOS' CUBE?
LIFE.
I HAVE CONTEMPLATED OUR SITUATION AND ARRIVED AT A PROFOUND TRUTH.
WOULD YOU CARE TO HEAR IT, MISTRESS?
YES.
THERE ARE NO CONSTANTS.
THEY COULD NO MORE KEEP US HERE FOREVER, THAN THEY COULD REMAIN FREE THEMSELVES...
THEY WILL FALL--ALL MEN DO.
AND WHAT FOLLOWS WILL BE A RECKONING.

"A PERFECT WORLD"

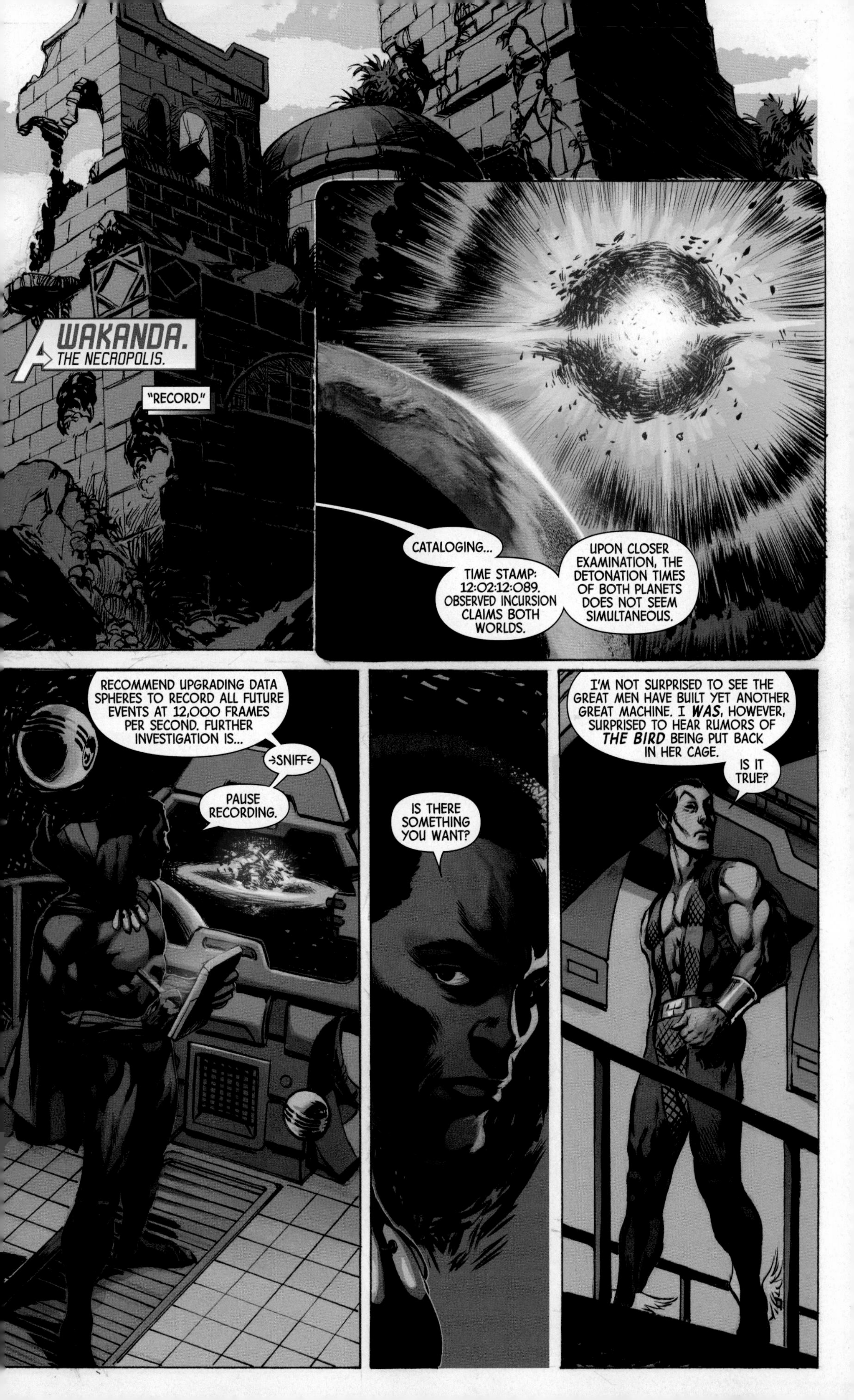
WAKANDA.
THE NECROPOLIS.
"RECORD."
CATALOGING...
TIME STAMP: 12:02:12:089. OBSERVED INCURSION CLAIMS BOTH WORLDS.
UPON CLOSER EXAMINATION, THE DETONATION TIMES OF BOTH PLANETS DOES NOT SEEM SIMULTANEOUS.
RECOMMEND UPGRADING DATA SPHERES TO RECORD ALL FUTURE EVENTS AT 12,000 FRAMES PER SECOND. FURTHER INVESTIGATION IS...
>SNIFF<
PAUSE RECORDING.
IS THERE SOMETHING YOU WANT?
I'M NOT SURPRISED TO SEE THE GREAT MEN HAVE BUILT YET ANOTHER GREAT MACHINE. I WAS, HOWEVER, SURPRISED TO HEAR RUMORS OF THE BIRD BEING PUT BACK IN HER CAGE.
IS IT TRUE?

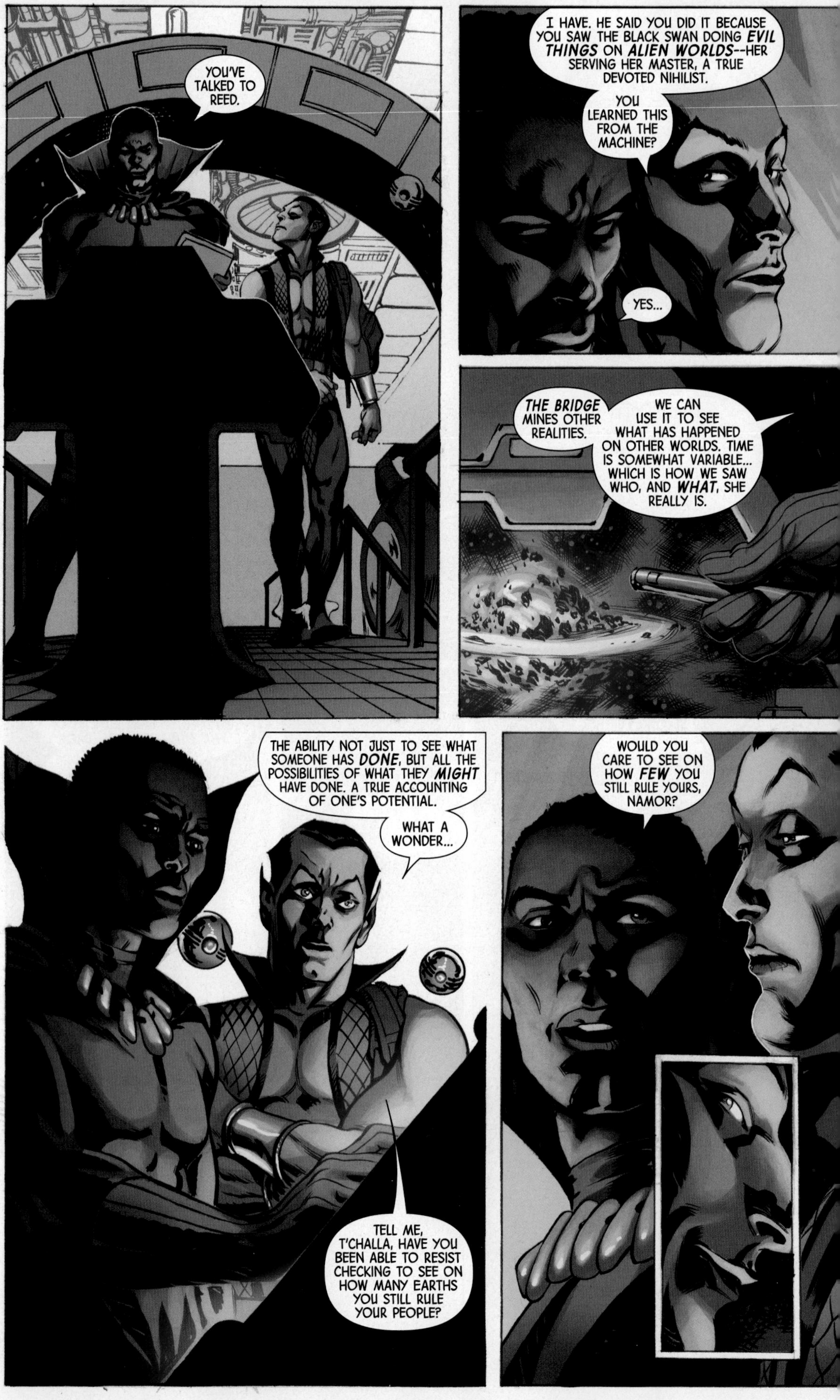
YOU'VE TALKED TO REED.
I HAVE. HE SAID YOU DID IT BECAUSE YOU SAW THE BLACK SWAN DOING EVIL THINGS ON ALIEN WORLDS--HER SERVING HER MASTER, A TRUE DEVOTED NIHILIST.
YOU LEARNED THIS FROM THE MACHINE?
YES...
THE BRIDGE MINES OTHER REALITIES.
WE CAN USE IT TO SEE WHAT HAS HAPPENED ON OTHER WORLDS. TIME IS SOMEWHAT VARIABLE... WHICH IS HOW WE SAW WHO, AND WHAT, SHE REALLY IS.
THE ABILITY NOT JUST TO SEE WHAT SOMEONE HAS DONE, BUT ALL THE POSSIBILITIES OF WHAT THEY MIGHT HAVE DONE. A TRUE ACCOUNTING OF ONE'S POTENTIAL.
WHAT A WONDER...
TELL ME, T'CHALLA, HAVE YOU BEEN ABLE TO RESIST CHECKING TO SEE ON HOW MANY EARTHS YOU STILL RULE YOUR PEOPLE?
WOULD YOU CARE TO SEE ON HOW FEW YOU STILL RULE YOURS, NAMOR?

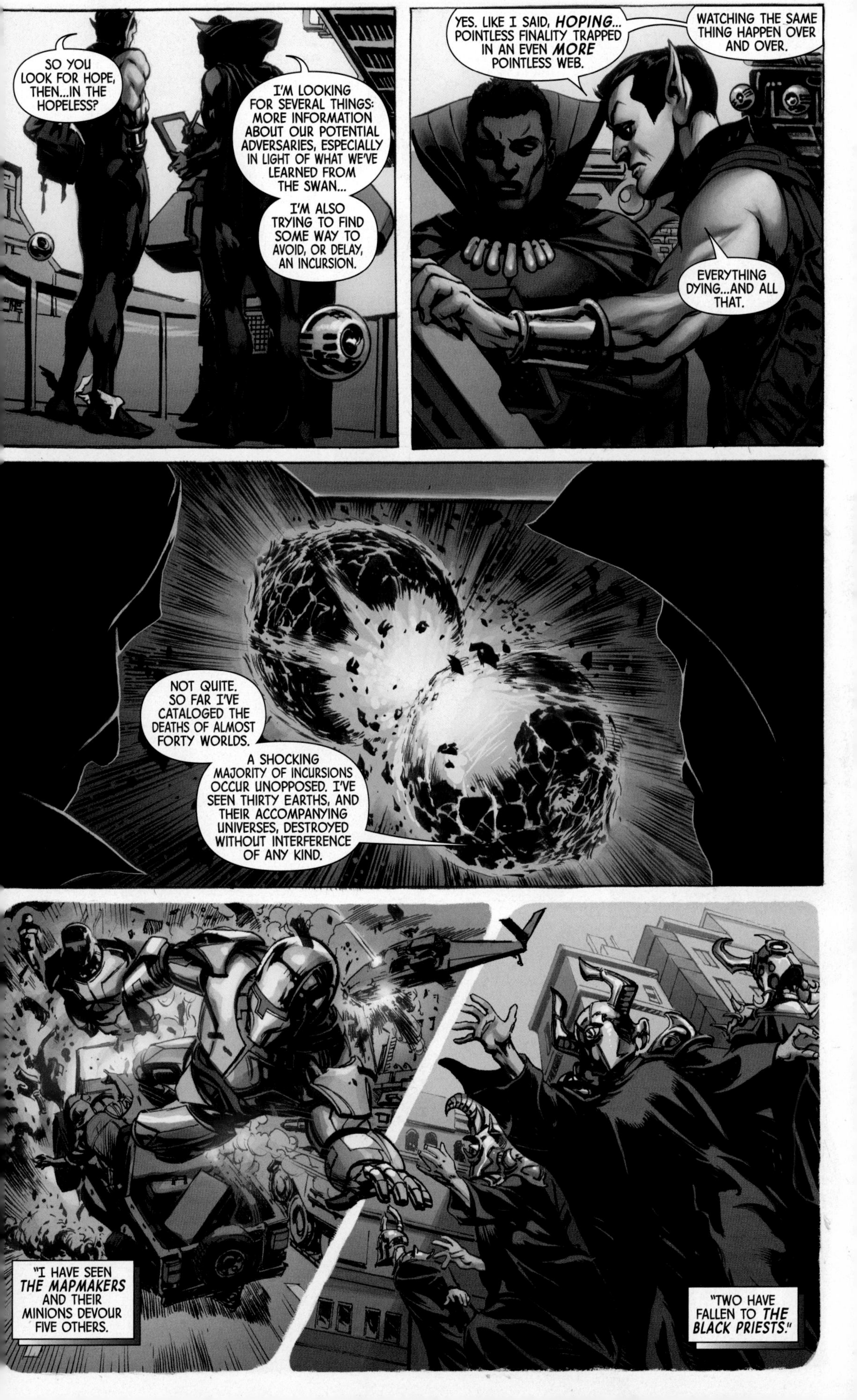
SO YOU LOOK FOR HOPE, THEN...IN THE HOPELESS?
I'M LOOKING FOR SEVERAL THINGS: MORE INFORMATION ABOUT OUR POTENTIAL ADVERSARIES, ESPECIALLY IN LIGHT OF WHAT WE'VE LEARNED FROM THE SWAN...
I'M ALSO TRYING TO FIND SOME WAY TO AVOID, OR DELAY, AN INCURSION.
YES. LIKE I SAID, HOPING... POINTLESS FINALITY TRAPPED IN AN EVEN MORE POINTLESS WEB.
WATCHING THE SAME THING HAPPEN OVER AND OVER.
EVERYTHING DYING...AND ALL THAT.
NOT QUITE. SO FAR I'VE CATALOGED THE DEATHS OF ALMOST FORTY WORLDS.
A SHOCKING MAJORITY OF INCURSIONS OCCUR UNOPPOSED. I'VE SEEN THIRTY EARTHS, AND THEIR ACCOMPANYING UNIVERSES, DESTROYED WITHOUT INTERFERENCE OF ANY KIND.
"I HAVE SEEN THE MAPMAKERS AND THEIR MINIONS DEVOUR FIVE OTHERS.
"TWO HAVE FALLEN TO THE BLACK PRIESTS."

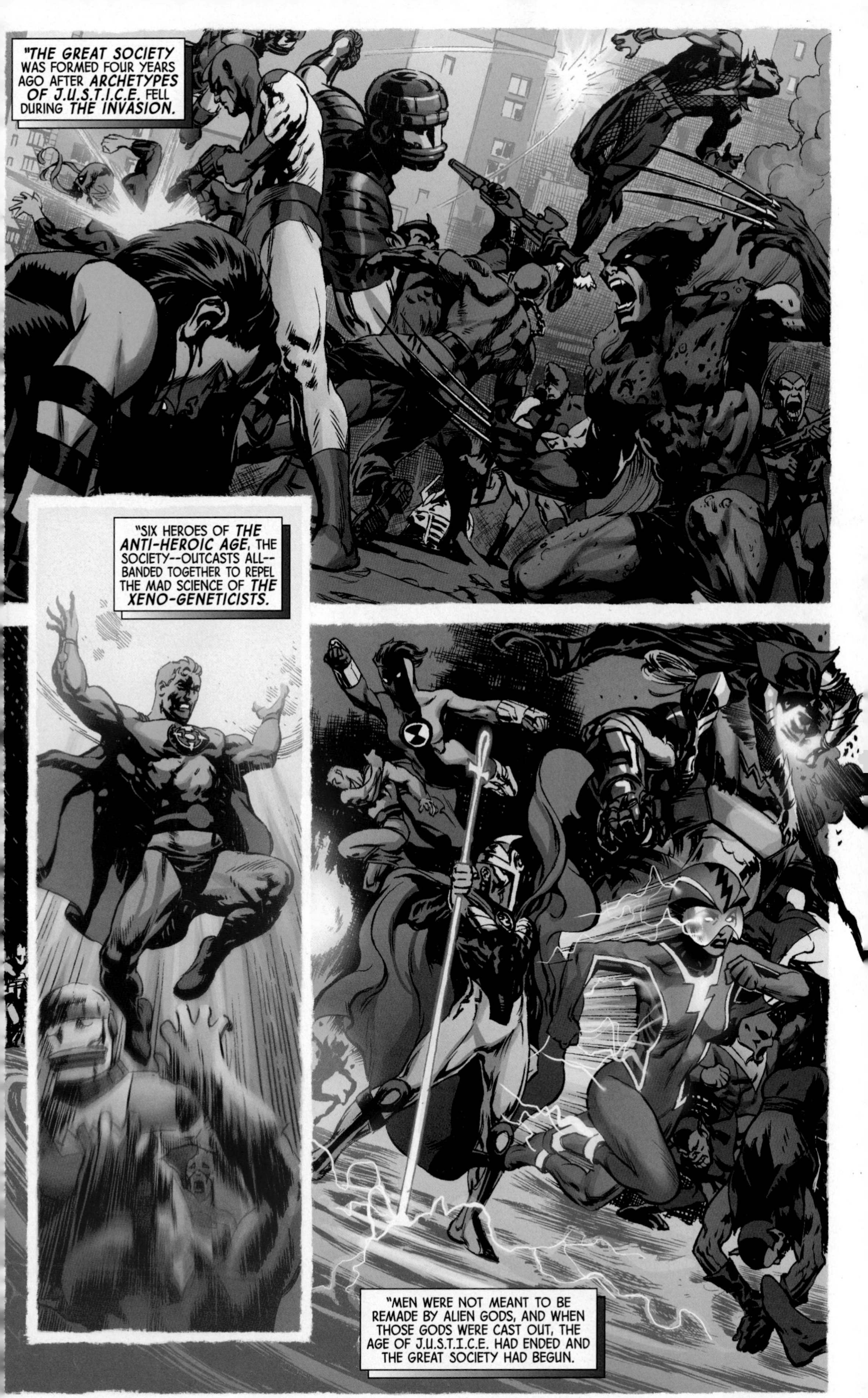
"THE GREAT SOCIETY WAS FORMED FOUR YEARS AGO AFTER ARCHETYPES OF J.U.S.T.I.C.E. FELL DURING THE INVASION.
"SIX HEROES OF THE ANTI-HEROIC AGE, THE SOCIETY--OUTCASTS ALL--BANDED TOGETHER TO REPEL THE MAD SCIENCE OF THE XENO-GENETICISTS.
"MEN WERE NOT MEANT TO BE REMADE BY ALIEN GODS, AND WHEN THOSE GODS WERE CAST OUT, THE AGE OF J.U.S.T.I.C.E. HAD ENDED AND THE GREAT SOCIETY HAD BEGUN.

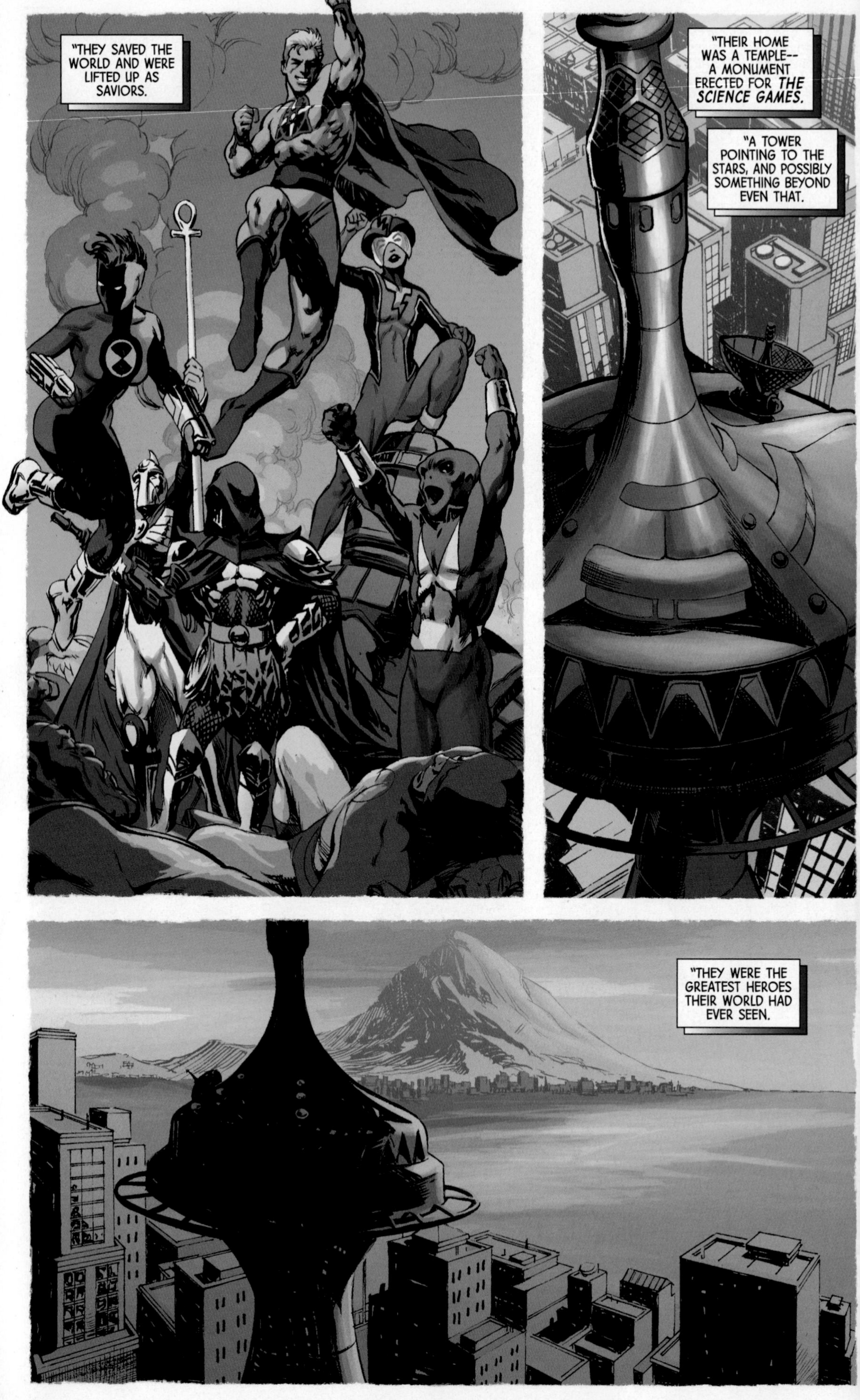
"THEY SAVED THE WORLD AND WERE LIFTED UP AS SAVIORS.
"THEIR HOME WAS A TEMPLE-- A MONUMENT ERECTED FOR THE SCIENCE GAMES.
"A TOWER POINTING TO THE STARS, AND POSSIBLY SOMETHING BEYOND EVEN THAT.
"THEY WERE THE GREATEST HEROES THEIR WORLD HAD EVER SEEN.

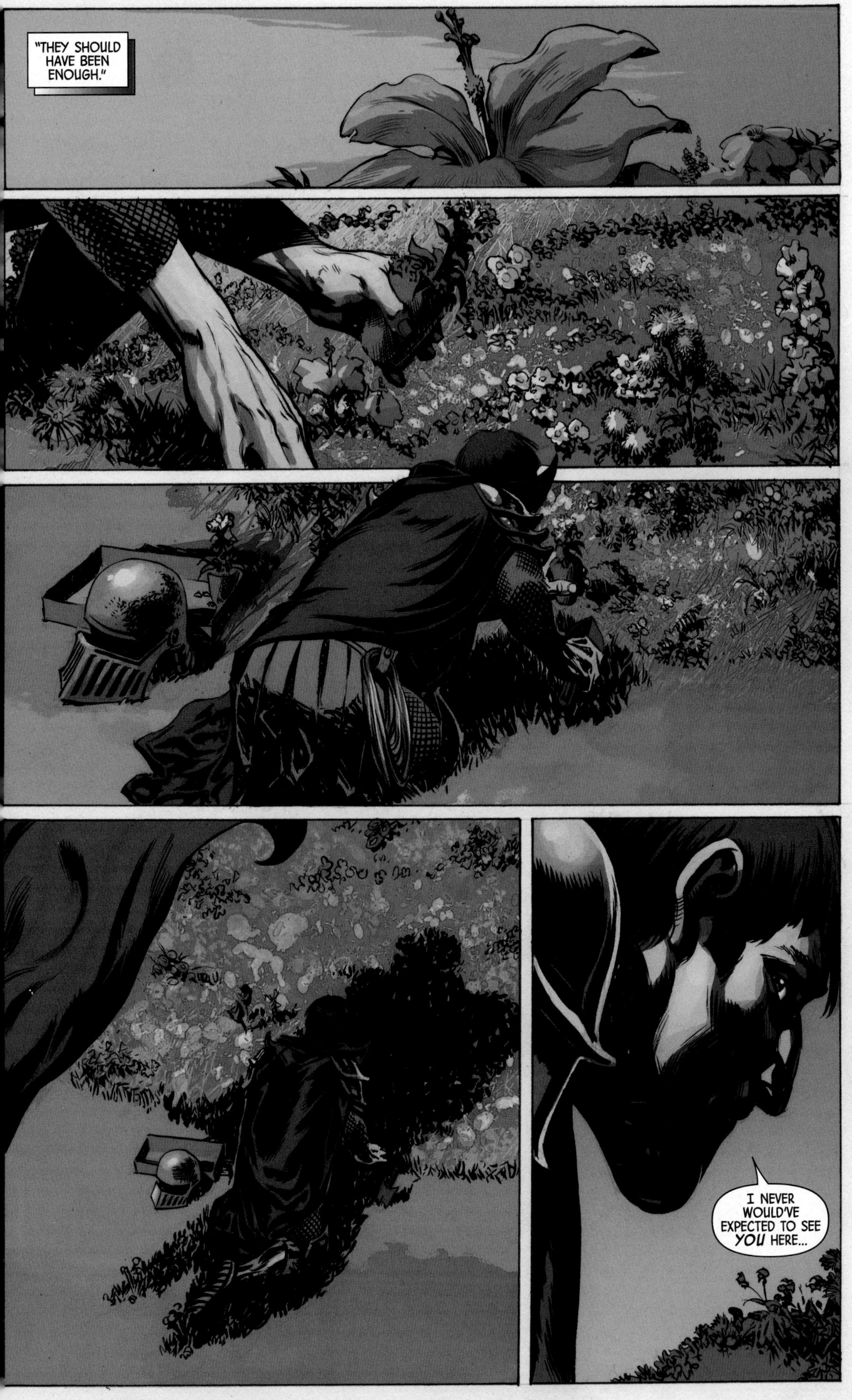
"THEY SHOULD HAVE BEEN ENOUGH."
I NEVER WOULD'VE EXPECTED TO SEE *YOU* HERE...

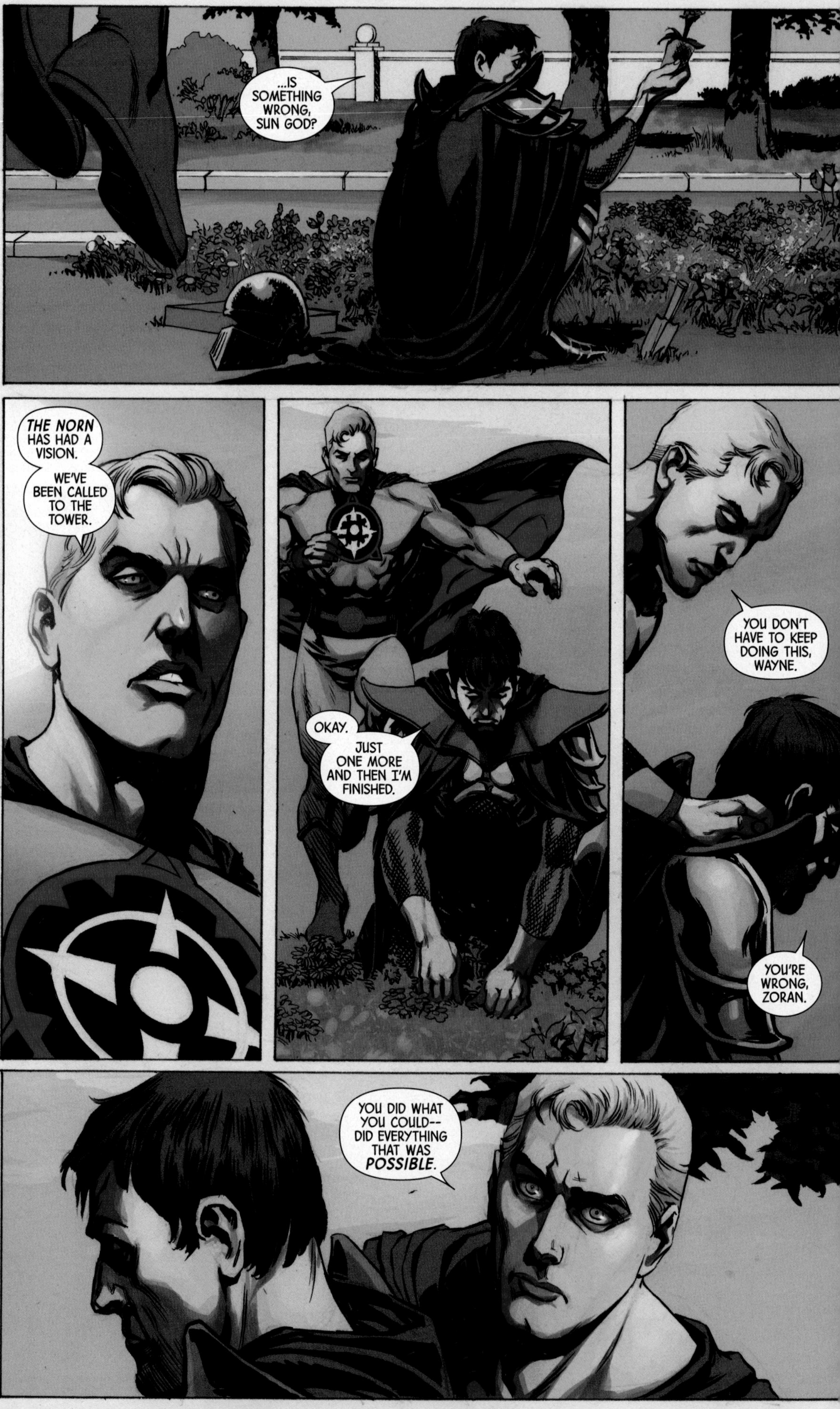
...IS SOMETHING WRONG, SUN GOD?
THE NORN HAS HAD A VISION.
WE'VE BEEN CALLED TO THE TOWER.
OKAY.
JUST ONE MORE AND THEN I'M FINISHED.
YOU DON'T HAVE TO KEEP DOING THIS, WAYNE.
YOU'RE WRONG, ZORAN.
YOU DID WHAT YOU COULD-- DID EVERYTHING THAT WAS *POSSIBLE*.

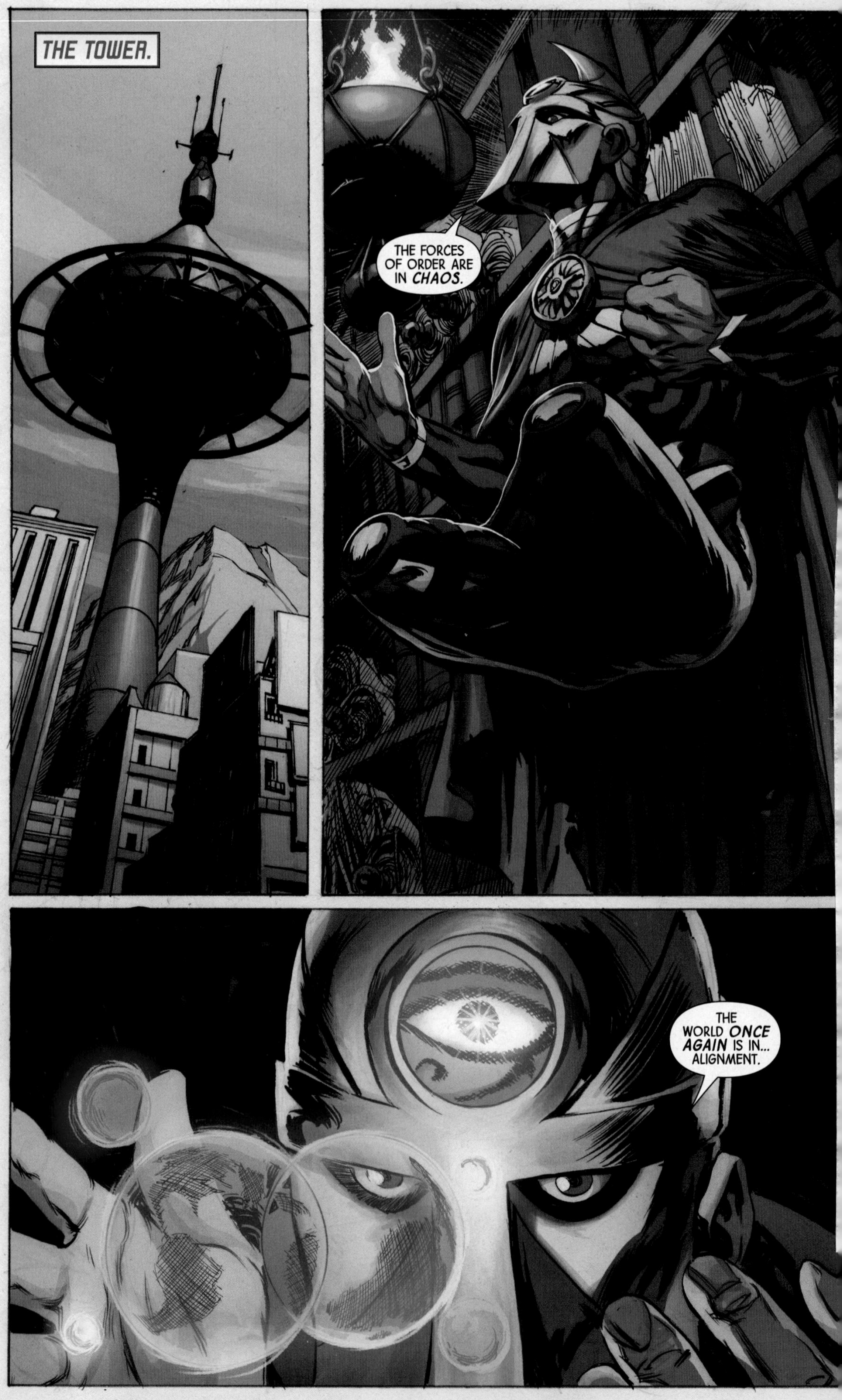
THE TOWER.
THE FORCES OF ORDER ARE IN CHAOS.
THE WORLD ONCE AGAIN IS IN... ALIGNMENT.

SO... INCURSION.

ANOTHER ONE.

I HAVE CHECKED THE ORBS. ALL THE SPHERES REMAIN UNFAZED EXCEPT THIS ONE.

UNLESS WE FALL.

THEN ALL THE SPHERES WILL SHATTER.

IT'S CONSISTENT. THE SAME EVERY TIME. I CAN FEEL THE HARMONICS FROM HERE...

PITCH AND FREQUENCY INCREASE.

THERE WILL BE MORE...AND SOON.

THEN WE'LL HAVE TO KEEP DOING WHAT WE'RE DOING...

AND DO IT UNTIL WE DIE.

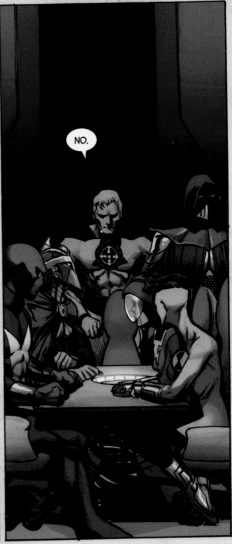

NO.

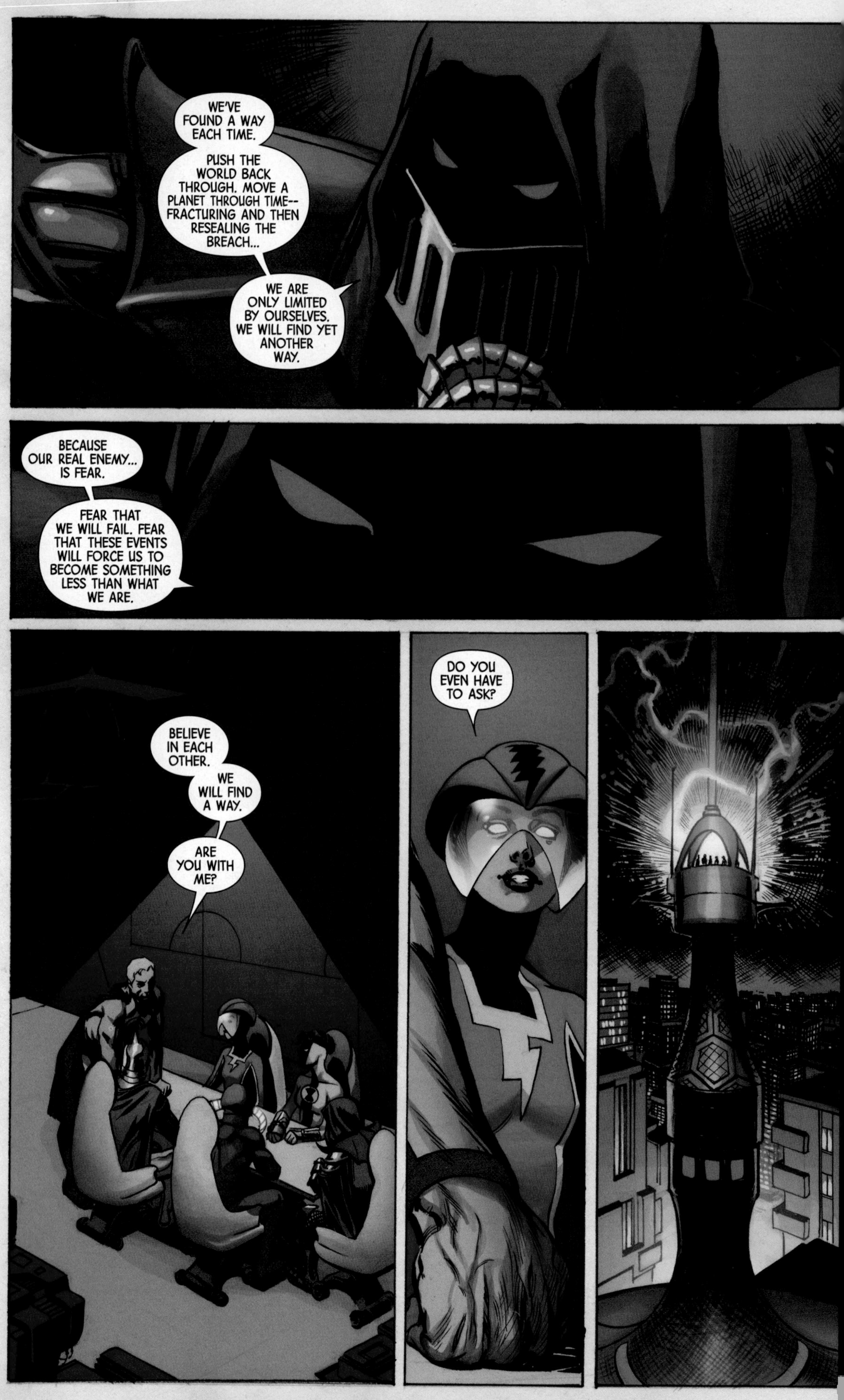
WE'VE FOUND A WAY EACH TIME.
PUSH THE WORLD BACK THROUGH. MOVE A PLANET THROUGH TIME--FRACTURING AND THEN RESEALING THE BREACH...
WE ARE ONLY LIMITED BY OURSELVES. WE WILL FIND YET ANOTHER WAY.
BECAUSE OUR REAL ENEMY... IS FEAR.
FEAR THAT WE WILL FAIL. FEAR THAT THESE EVENTS WILL FORCE US TO BECOME SOMETHING LESS THAN WHAT WE ARE.
BELIEVE IN EACH OTHER.
WE WILL FIND A WAY.
ARE YOU WITH ME?
DO YOU EVEN HAVE TO ASK?

THE WALL MUST BE CLOSE.

IT'S HERE. I CAN FEEL IT.

YEAH. FOUND IT.

READY?

YES. LET'S GO.

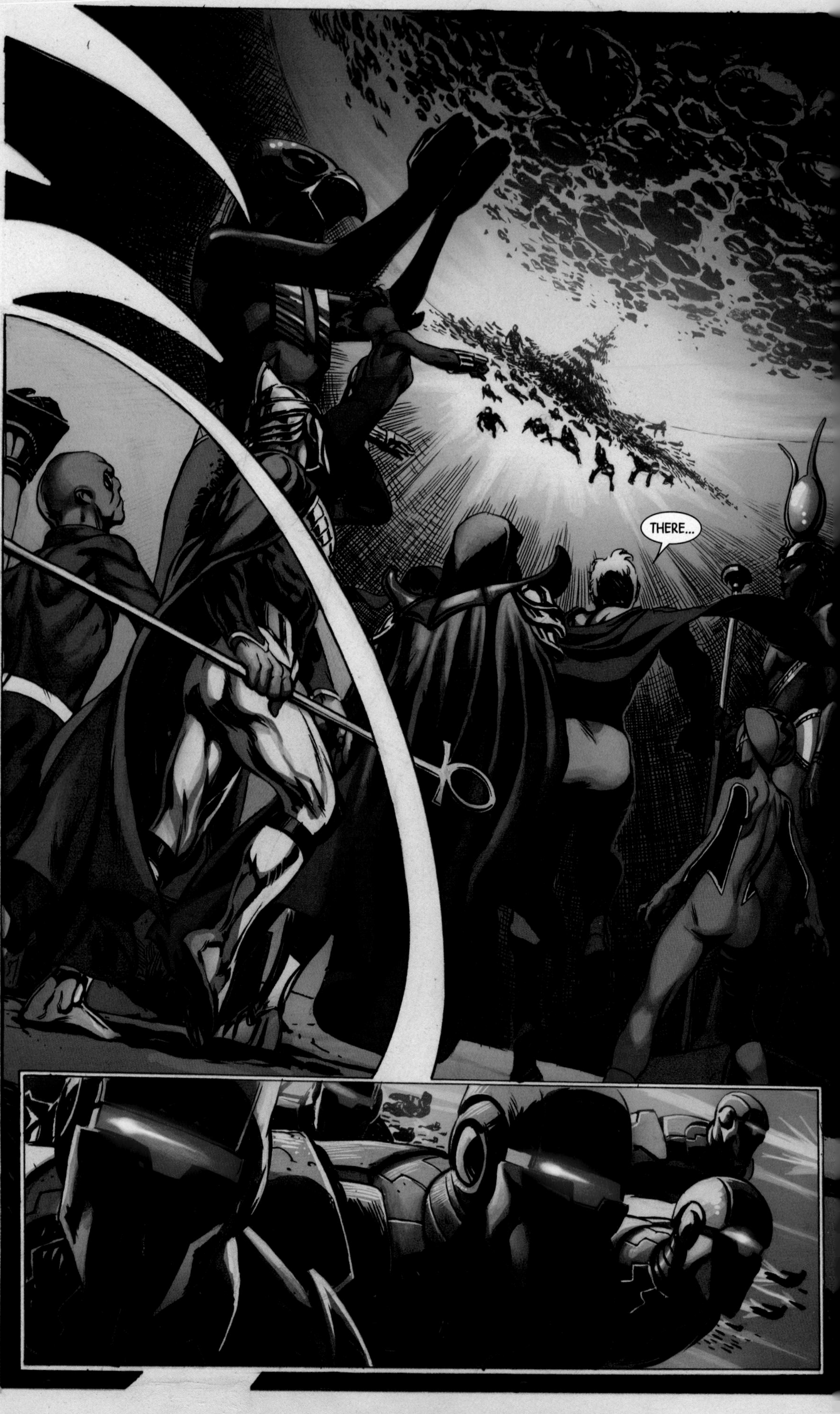
THERE...

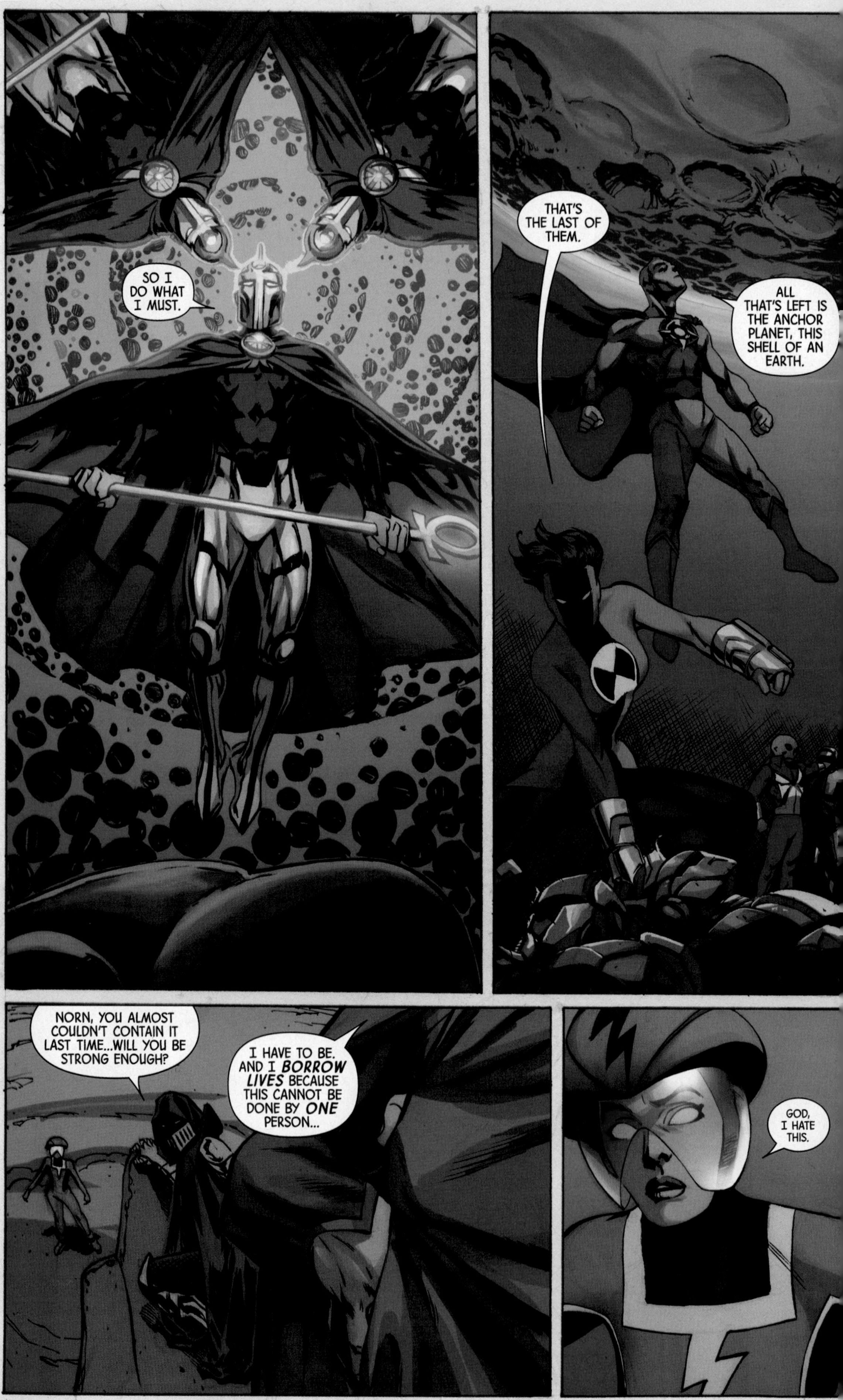
SO I DO WHAT I MUST.
THAT'S THE LAST OF THEM.
ALL THAT'S LEFT IS THE ANCHOR PLANET, THIS SHELL OF AN EARTH.
NORN, YOU ALMOST COULDN'T CONTAIN IT LAST TIME...WILL YOU BE STRONG ENOUGH?
I HAVE TO BE. AND I *BORROW LIVES* BECAUSE THIS CANNOT BE DONE BY *ONE* PERSON...
GOD, I HATE THIS.

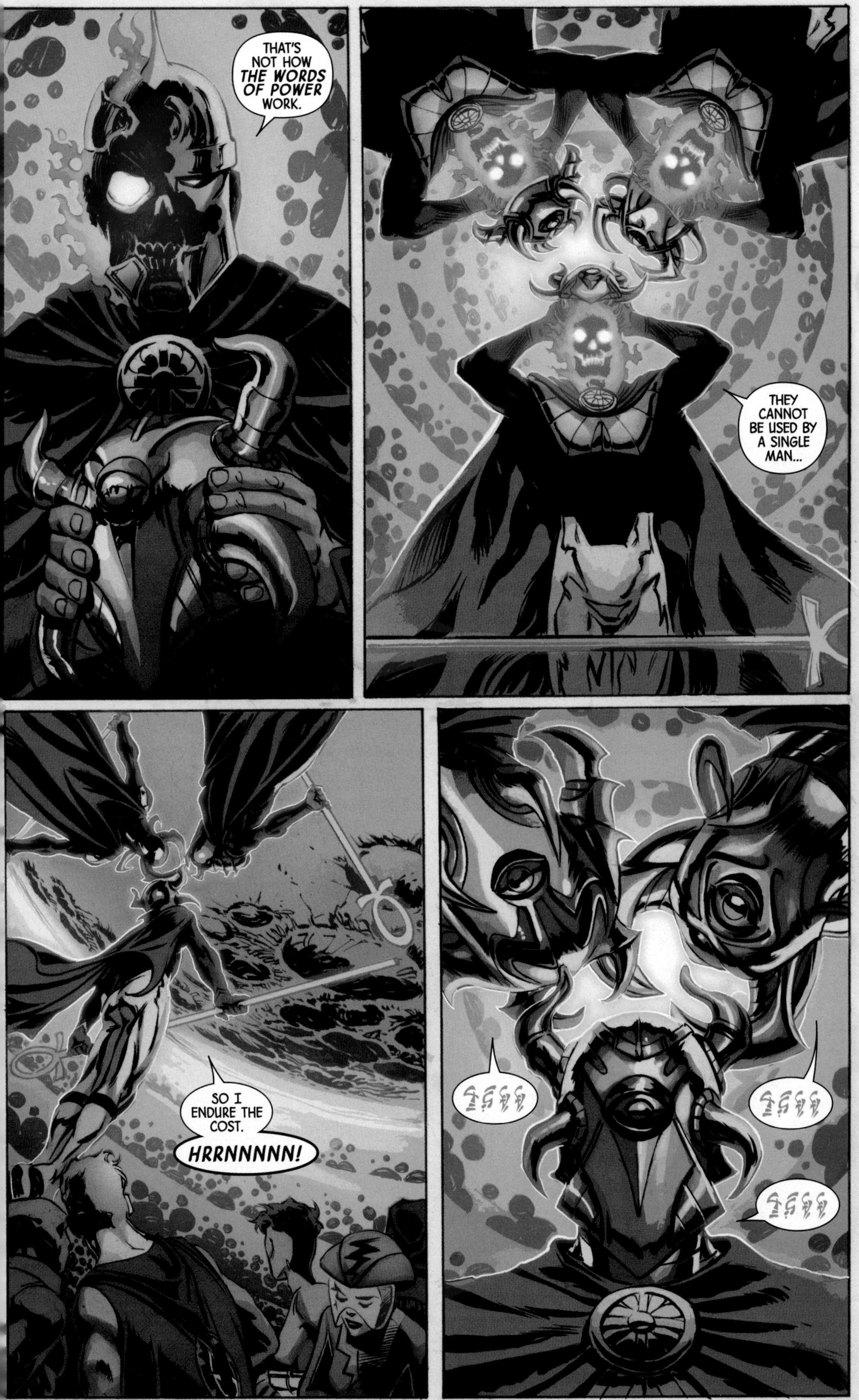
THAT'S NOT HOW *THE WORDS OF POWER* WORK.
THEY CANNOT BE USED BY A SINGLE MAN...
SO I ENDURE THE COST.
HRRNNNNN!

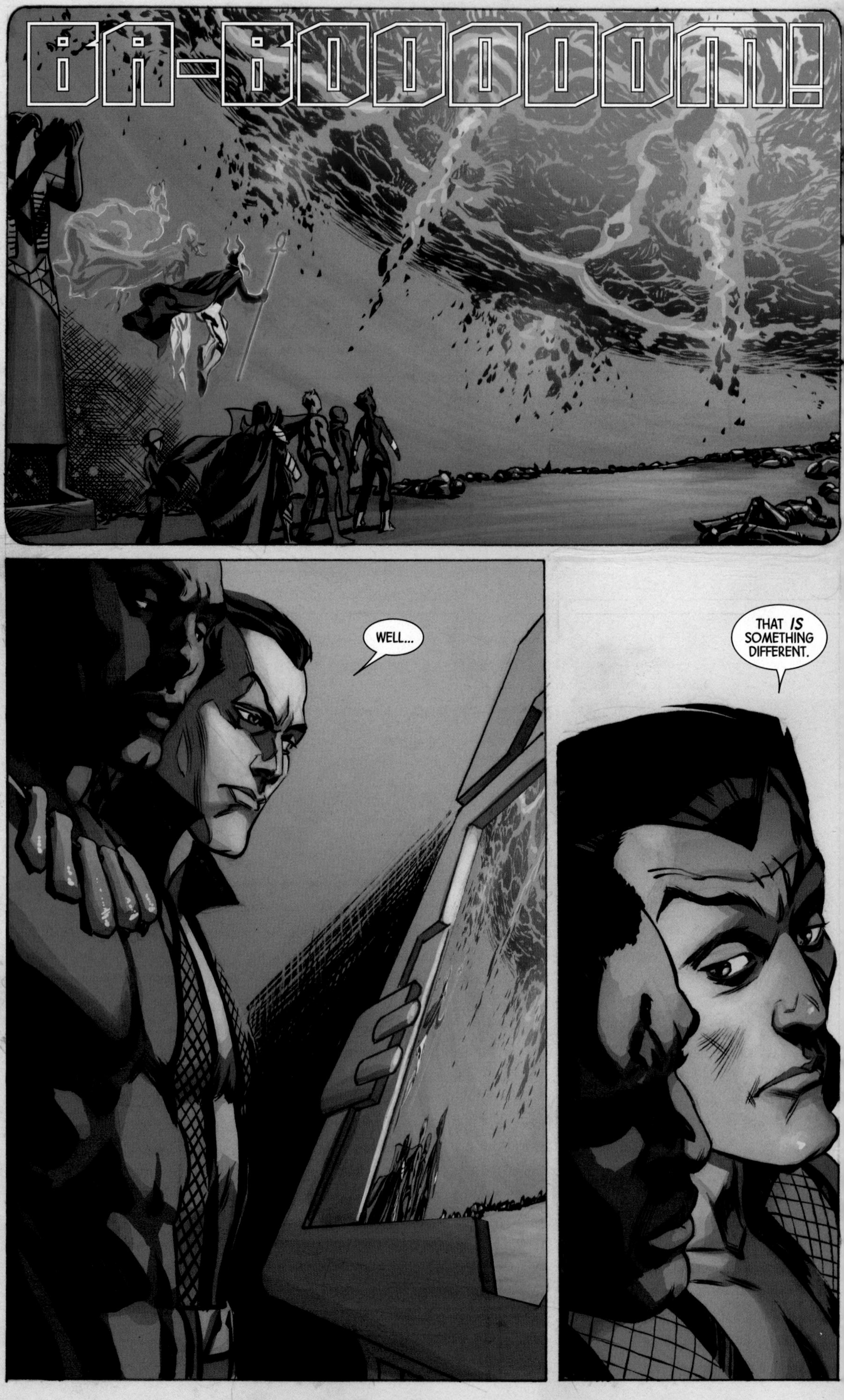

BA-BOOOOOM!
WELL...
THAT *IS* SOMETHING DIFFERENT.

"A PERFECT WORLD II"

PREVIOUSLY IN
THE GREAT SOCIETY

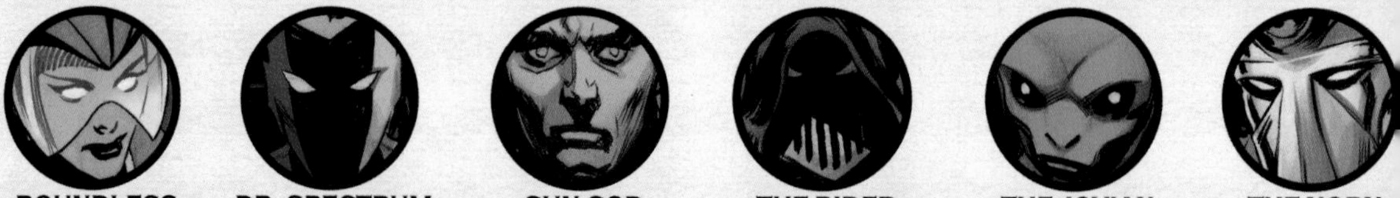

BOUNDLESS DR. SPECTRUM SUN GOD THE RIDER THE JOVIAN THE NORN

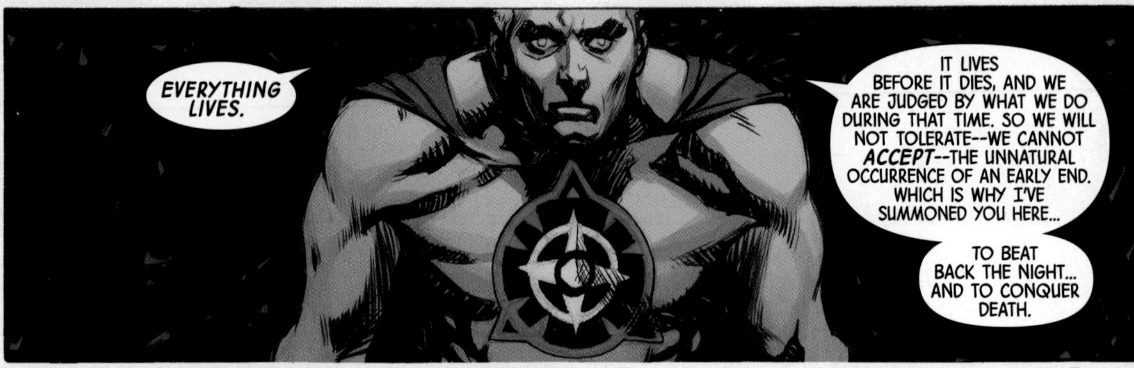
EVERYTHING LIVES.
IT LIVES BEFORE IT DIES, AND WE ARE JUDGED BY WHAT WE DO DURING THAT TIME. SO WE WILL NOT TOLERATE--WE CANNOT ACCEPT--THE UNNATURAL OCCURRENCE OF AN EARLY END. WHICH IS WHY I'VE SUMMONED YOU HERE...
TO BEAT BACK THE NIGHT... AND TO CONQUER DEATH.

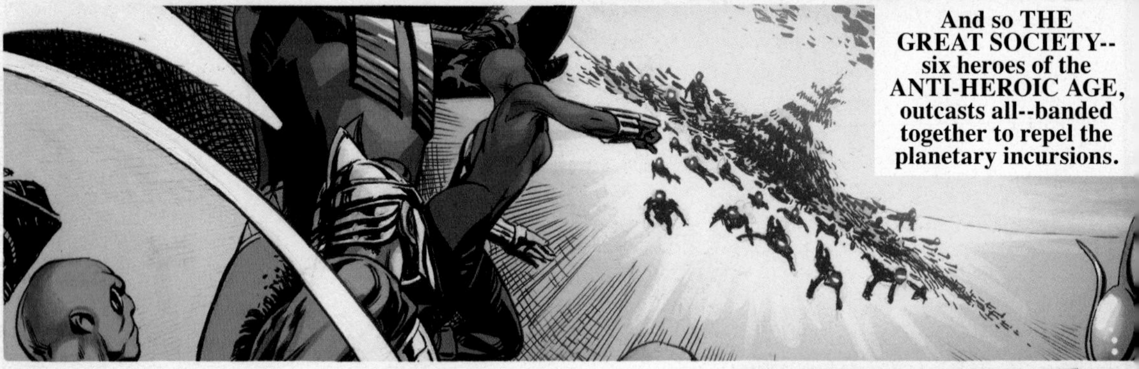
And so THE GREAT SOCIETY--six heroes of the ANTI-HEROIC AGE, outcasts all--banded together to repel the planetary incursions.

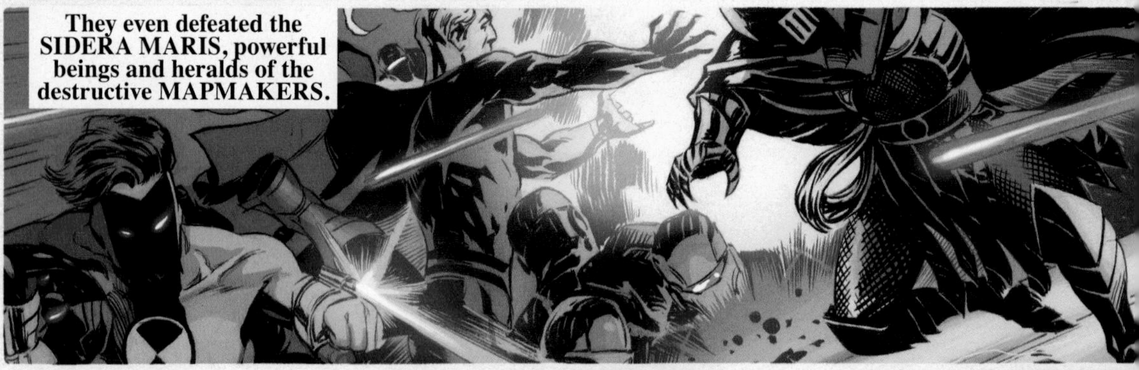
They even defeated the SIDERA MARIS, powerful beings and heralds of the destructive MAPMAKERS.

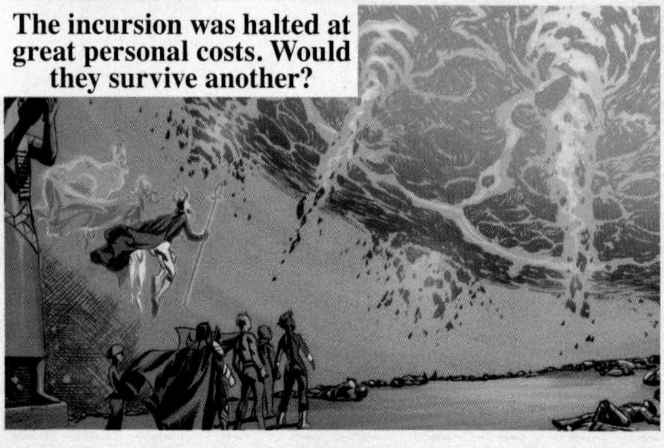
The incursion was halted at great personal costs. Would they survive another?

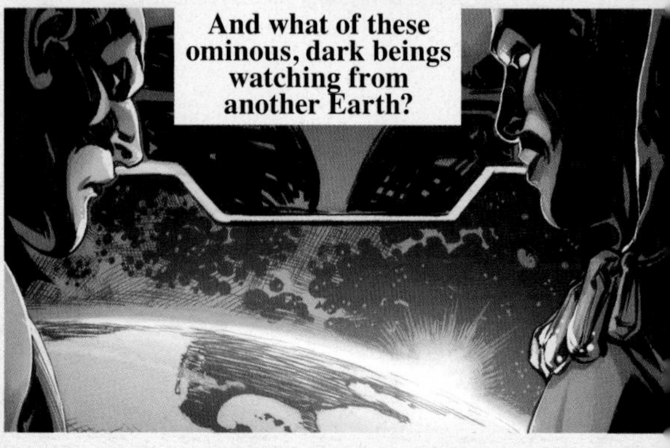
And what of these ominous, dark beings watching from another Earth?

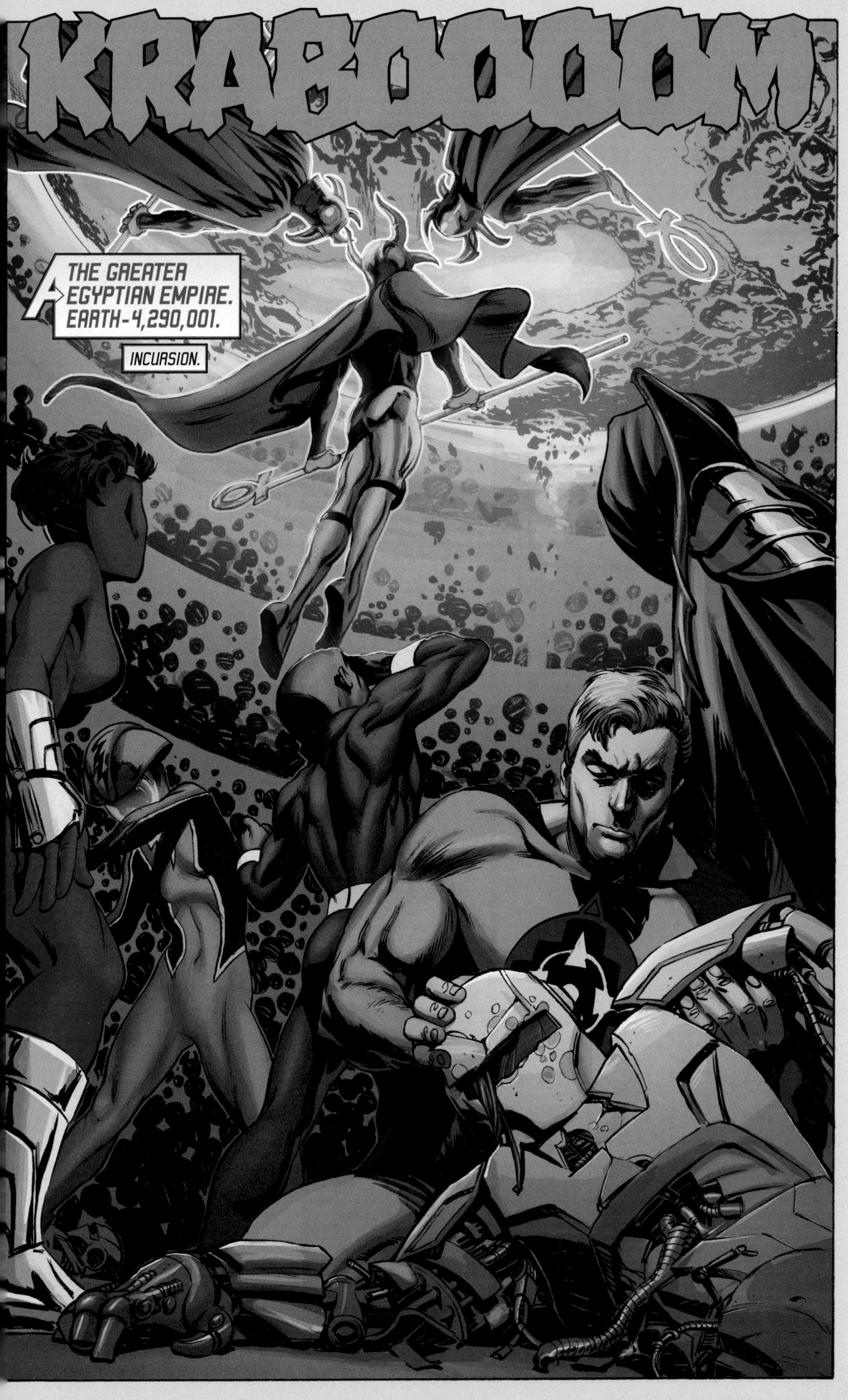
KRABOOOOM
THE GREATER EGYPTIAN EMPIRE. EARTH-4,290,001.
INCURSION.

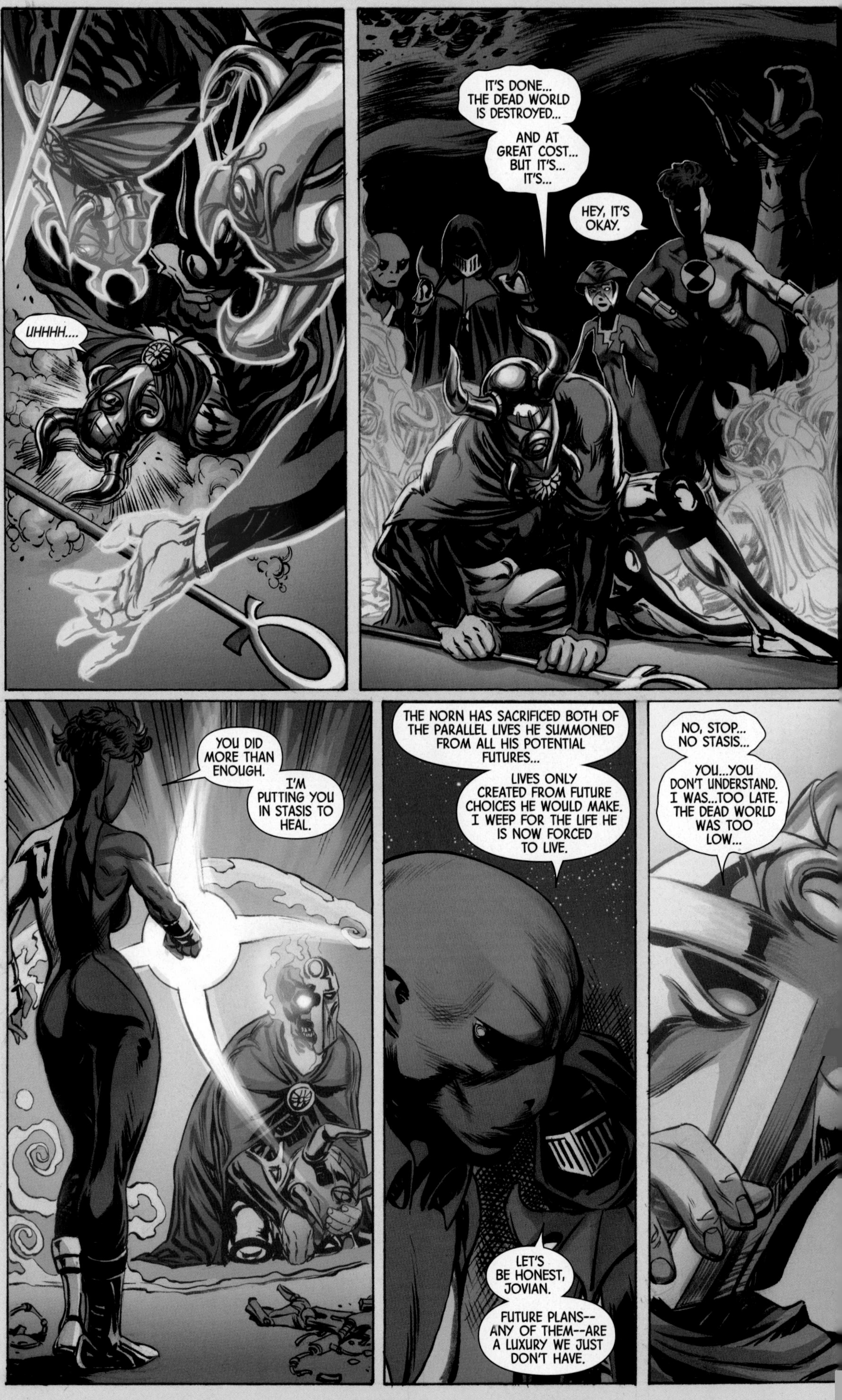
UHHHH....
IT'S DONE... THE DEAD WORLD IS DESTROYED...
AND AT GREAT COST... BUT IT'S... IT'S...
HEY, IT'S OKAY.
YOU DID MORE THAN ENOUGH.
I'M PUTTING YOU IN STASIS TO HEAL.
THE NORN HAS SACRIFICED BOTH OF THE PARALLEL LIVES HE SUMMONED FROM ALL HIS POTENTIAL FUTURES...
LIVES ONLY CREATED FROM FUTURE CHOICES HE WOULD MAKE. I WEEP FOR THE LIFE HE IS NOW FORCED TO LIVE.
LET'S BE HONEST, JOVIAN.
FUTURE PLANS--ANY OF THEM--ARE A LUXURY WE JUST DON'T HAVE.
NO, STOP... NO STASIS...
YOU...YOU DON'T UNDERSTAND. I WAS...TOO LATE. THE DEAD WORLD WAS TOO LOW...

NEW WORLDS.

NEVER ENOUGH WORLDS.

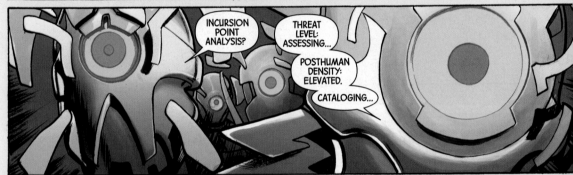

INCURSION POINT ANALYSIS?

THREAT LEVEL: ASSESSING...

POSTHUMAN DENSITY: ELEVATED.

CATALOGING...

MAPMAKERS! FOUR OF THEM!

BOUNDLESS! QUICKLY, BEFORE THEY CAN ADAPT AND--

ALREADY.

ON IT.

BOSS.

ADAPTATION OCCURS...

...IN THE CENTRAL A.I.

IF I CAN ACCESS IT...

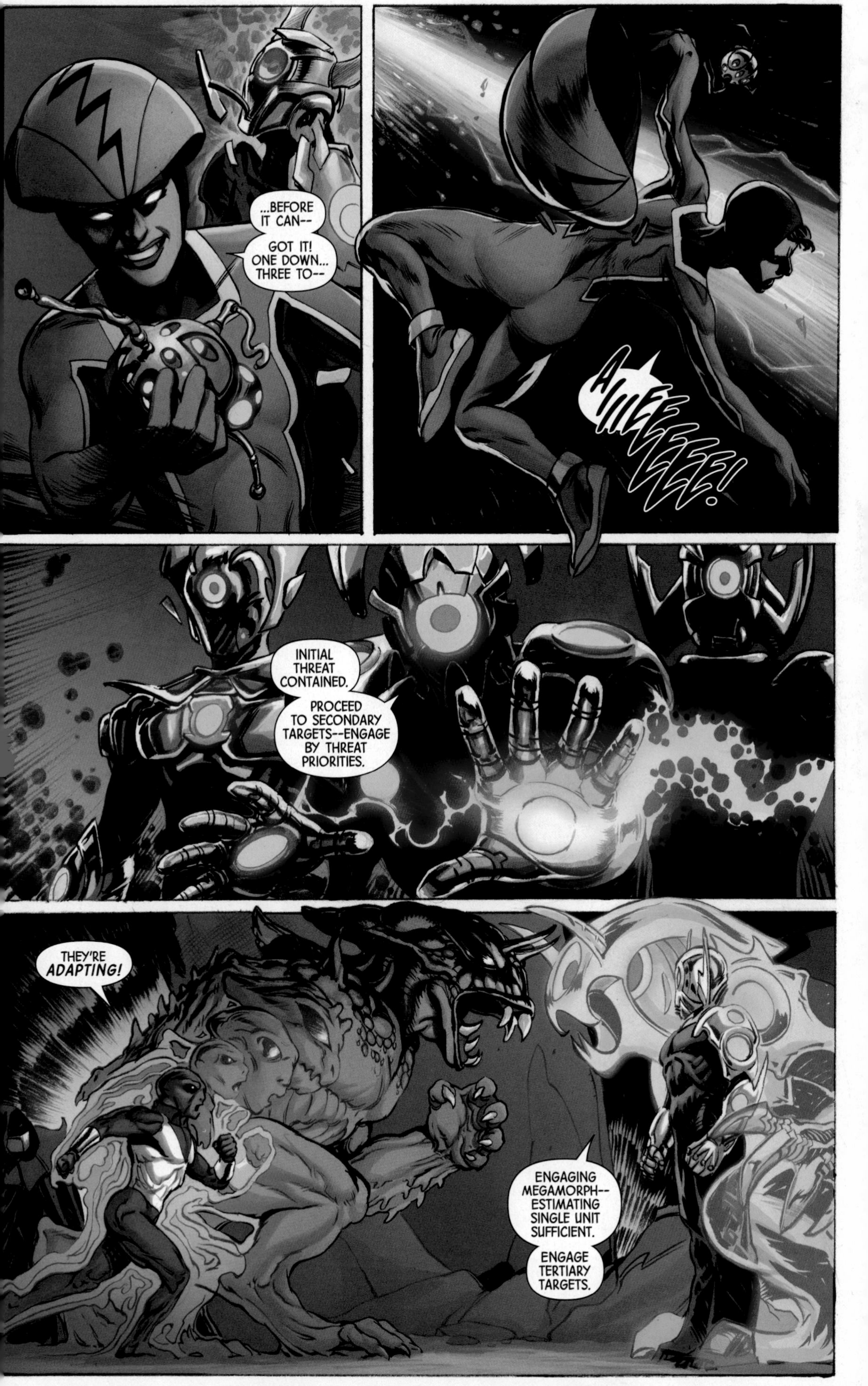
...BEFORE IT CAN--
GOT IT! ONE DOWN... THREE TO--
AIIEEEEEE!
INITIAL THREAT CONTAINED.
PROCEED TO SECONDARY TARGETS--ENGAGE BY THREAT PRIORITIES.
THEY'RE *ADAPTING!*
ENGAGING MEGAMORPH--ESTIMATING SINGLE UNIT SUFFICIENT.
ENGAGE TERTIARY TARGETS.

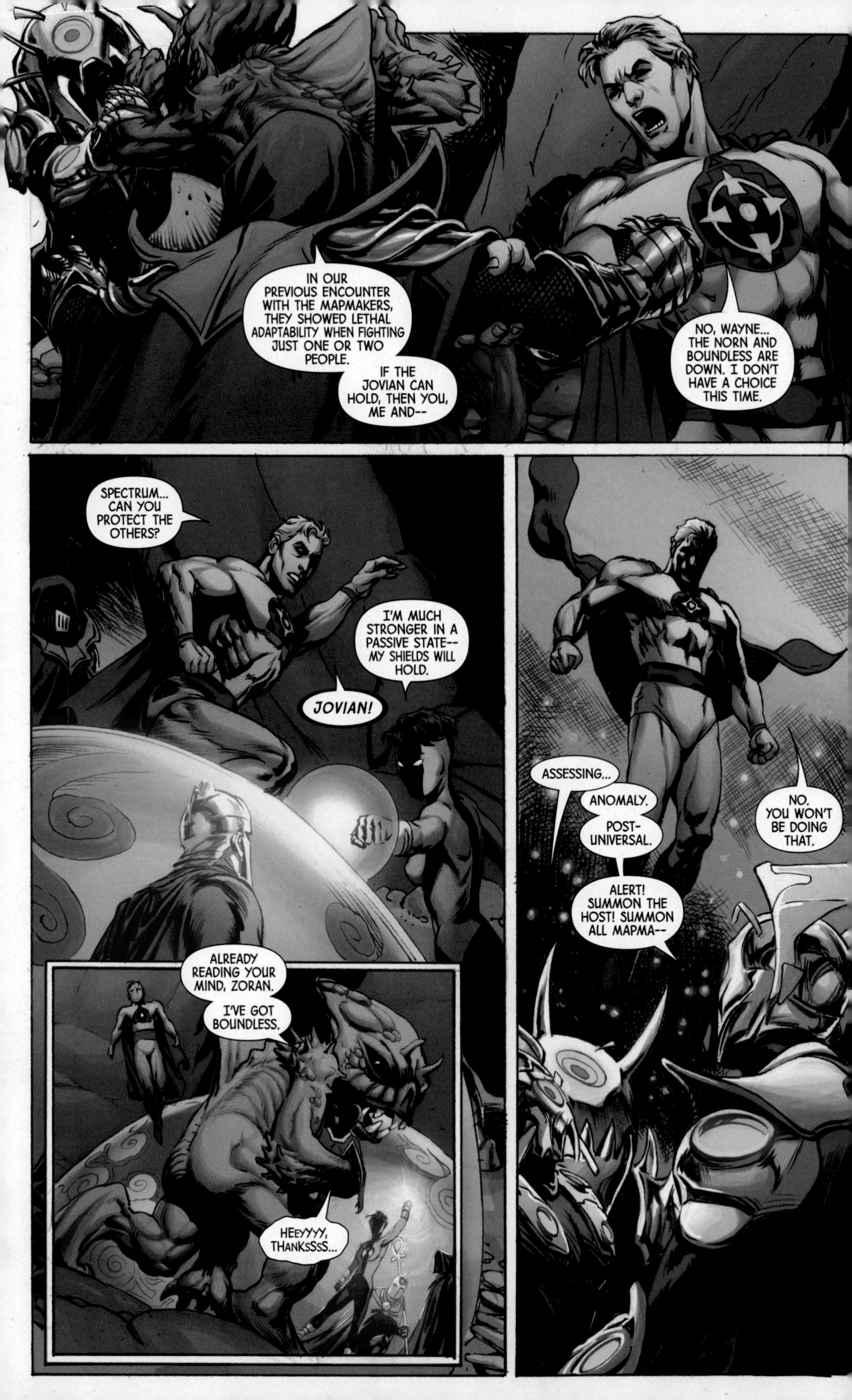
IN OUR PREVIOUS ENCOUNTER WITH THE MAPMAKERS, THEY SHOWED LETHAL ADAPTABILITY WHEN FIGHTING JUST ONE OR TWO PEOPLE.
IF THE JOVIAN CAN HOLD, THEN YOU, ME AND--
NO, WAYNE... THE NORN AND BOUNDLESS ARE DOWN. I DON'T HAVE A CHOICE THIS TIME.
SPECTRUM... CAN YOU PROTECT THE OTHERS?
I'M MUCH STRONGER IN A PASSIVE STATE-- MY SHIELDS WILL HOLD.
JOVIAN!
ALREADY READING YOUR MIND, ZORAN.
I'VE GOT BOUNDLESS.
HEEYYYY, THANKSSSS...
ASSESSING...
ANOMALY.
POST-UNIVERSAL.
ALERT! SUMMON THE HOST! SUMMON ALL MAPMA--
NO. YOU WON'T BE DOING THAT.

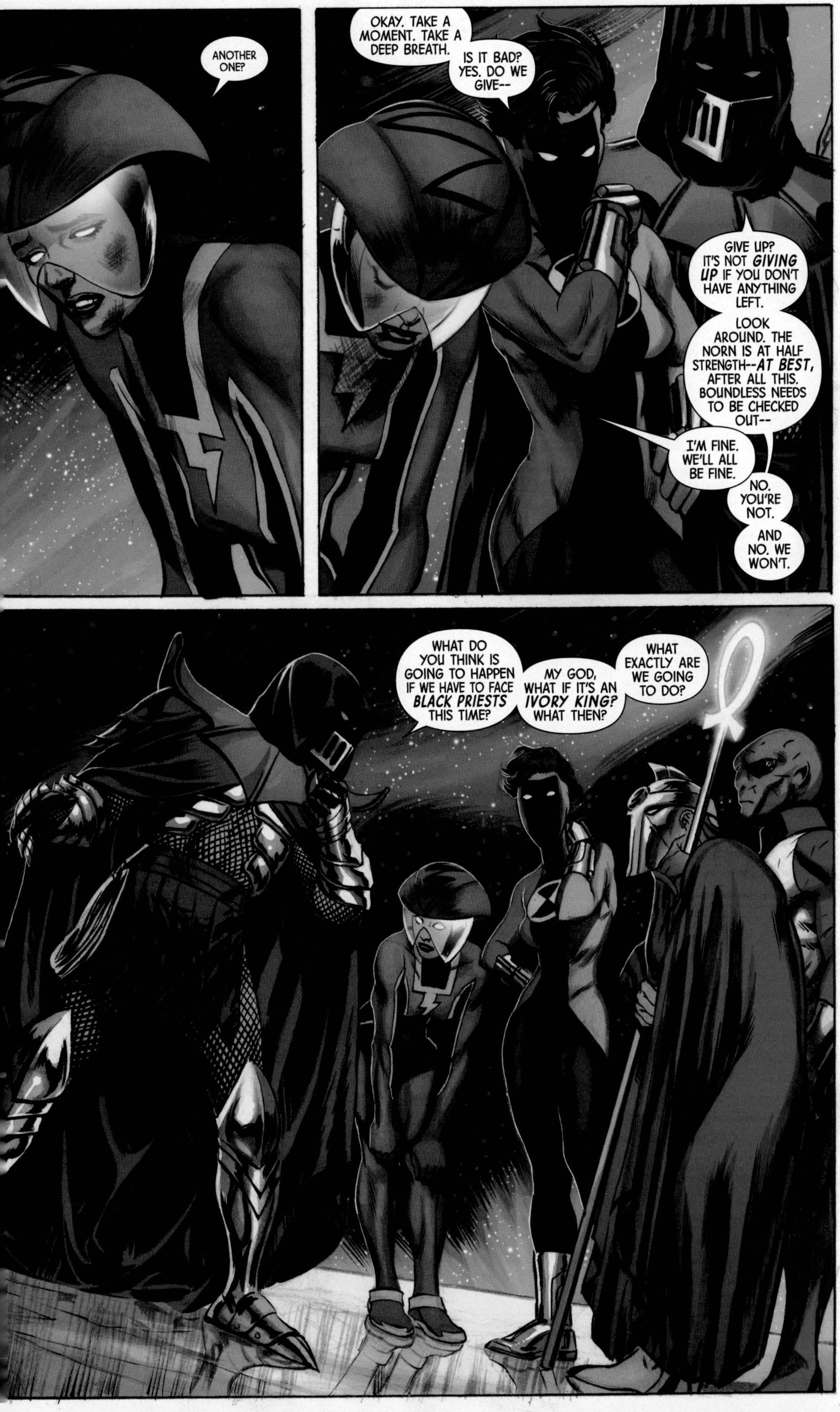
ANOTHER ONE?
OKAY. TAKE A MOMENT. TAKE A DEEP BREATH.
IS IT BAD? YES. DO WE GIVE--
GIVE UP? IT'S NOT GIVING UP IF YOU DON'T HAVE ANYTHING LEFT.
LOOK AROUND. THE NORN IS AT HALF STRENGTH--AT BEST, AFTER ALL THIS. BOUNDLESS NEEDS TO BE CHECKED OUT--
I'M FINE. WE'LL ALL BE FINE.
NO. YOU'RE NOT.
AND NO. WE WON'T.
WHAT DO YOU THINK IS GOING TO HAPPEN IF WE HAVE TO FACE BLACK PRIESTS THIS TIME?
MY GOD, WHAT IF IT'S AN IVORY KING? WHAT THEN?
WHAT EXACTLY ARE WE GOING TO DO?

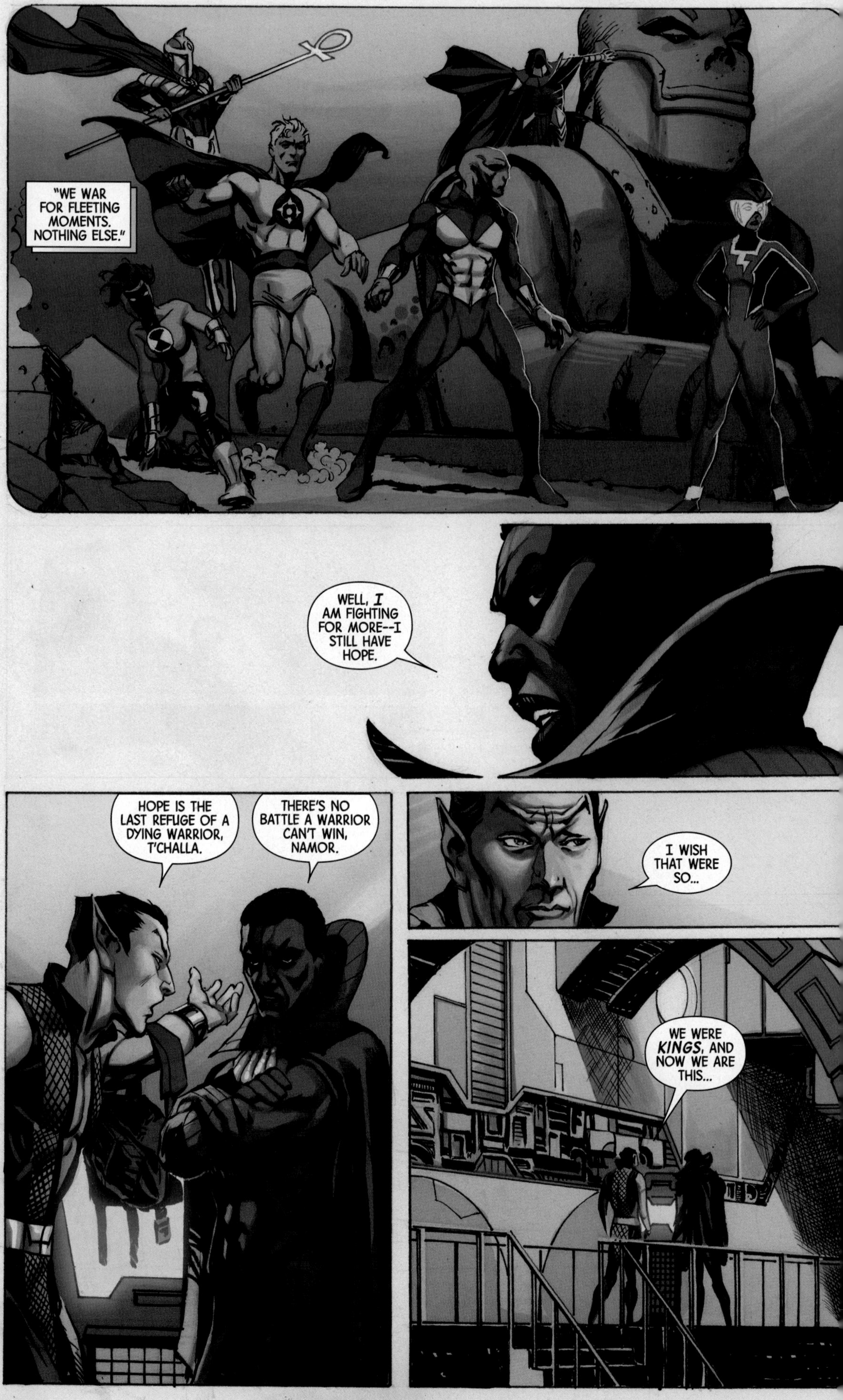
"WE WAR FOR FLEETING MOMENTS. NOTHING ELSE."
WELL, *I* AM FIGHTING FOR MORE--I STILL HAVE HOPE.
HOPE IS THE LAST REFUGE OF A DYING WARRIOR, T'CHALLA.
THERE'S NO BATTLE A WARRIOR CAN'T WIN, NAMOR.
I WISH THAT WERE SO...
WE WERE *KINGS*, AND NOW WE ARE THIS...

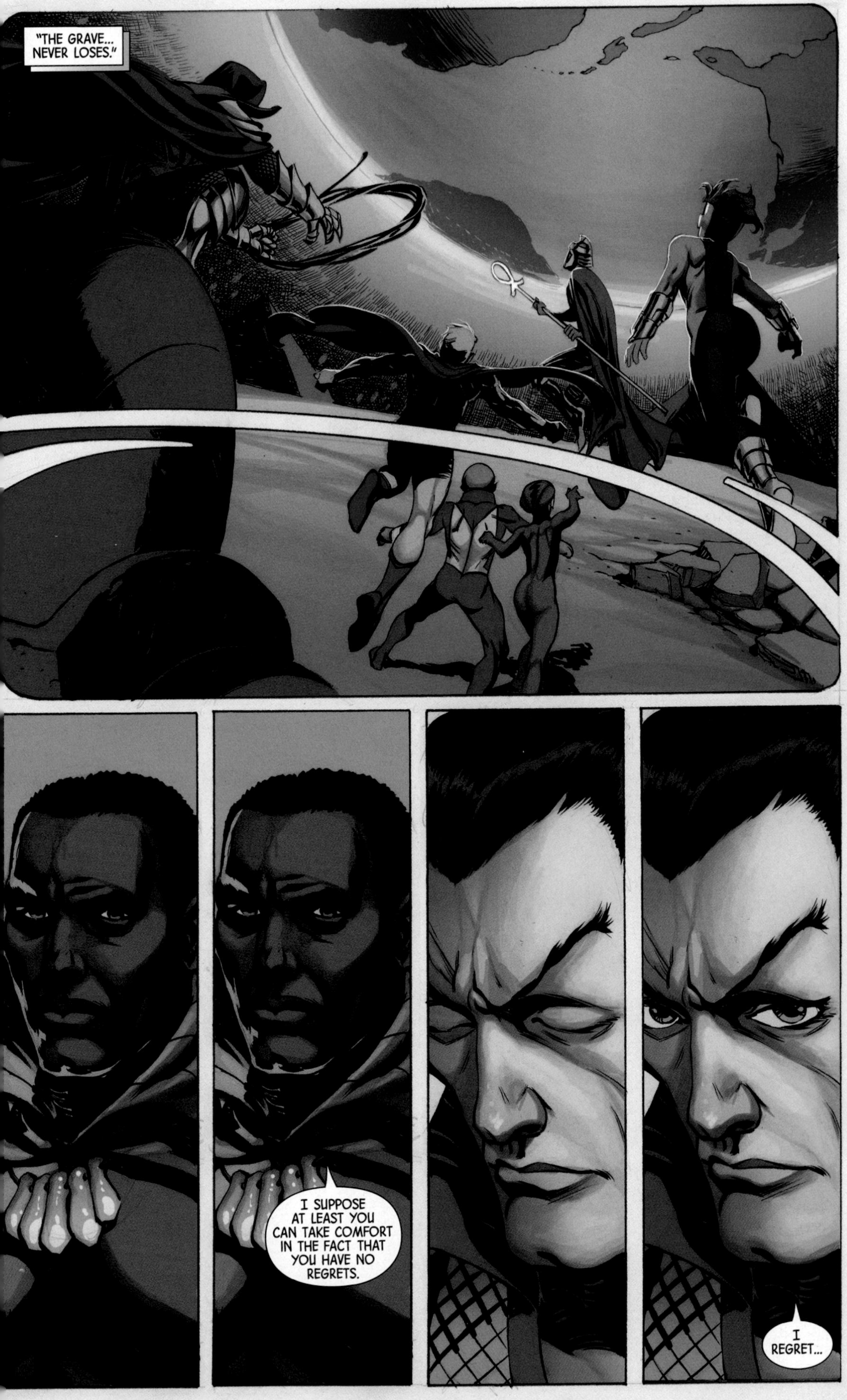
"THE GRAVE... NEVER LOSES."
I SUPPOSE AT LEAST YOU CAN TAKE COMFORT IN THE FACT THAT YOU HAVE NO REGRETS.
I REGRET...

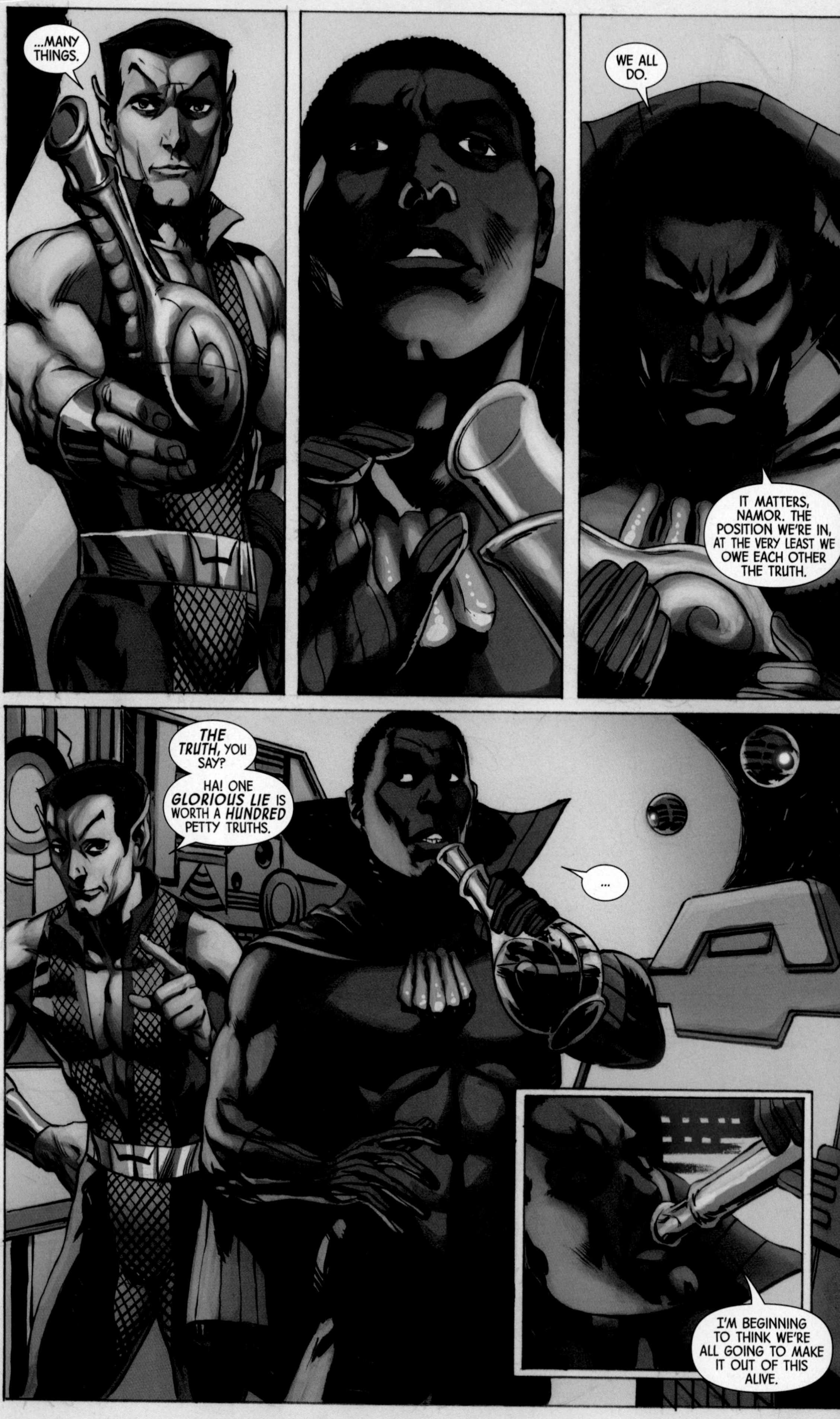
...MANY THINGS.
WE ALL DO.
IT MATTERS, NAMOR. THE POSITION WE'RE IN, AT THE VERY LEAST WE OWE EACH OTHER THE TRUTH.
THE TRUTH, YOU SAY?
HA! ONE *GLORIOUS LIE* IS WORTH A *HUNDRED* PETTY TRUTHS.
...
I'M BEGINNING TO THINK WE'RE ALL GOING TO MAKE IT OUT OF THIS ALIVE.

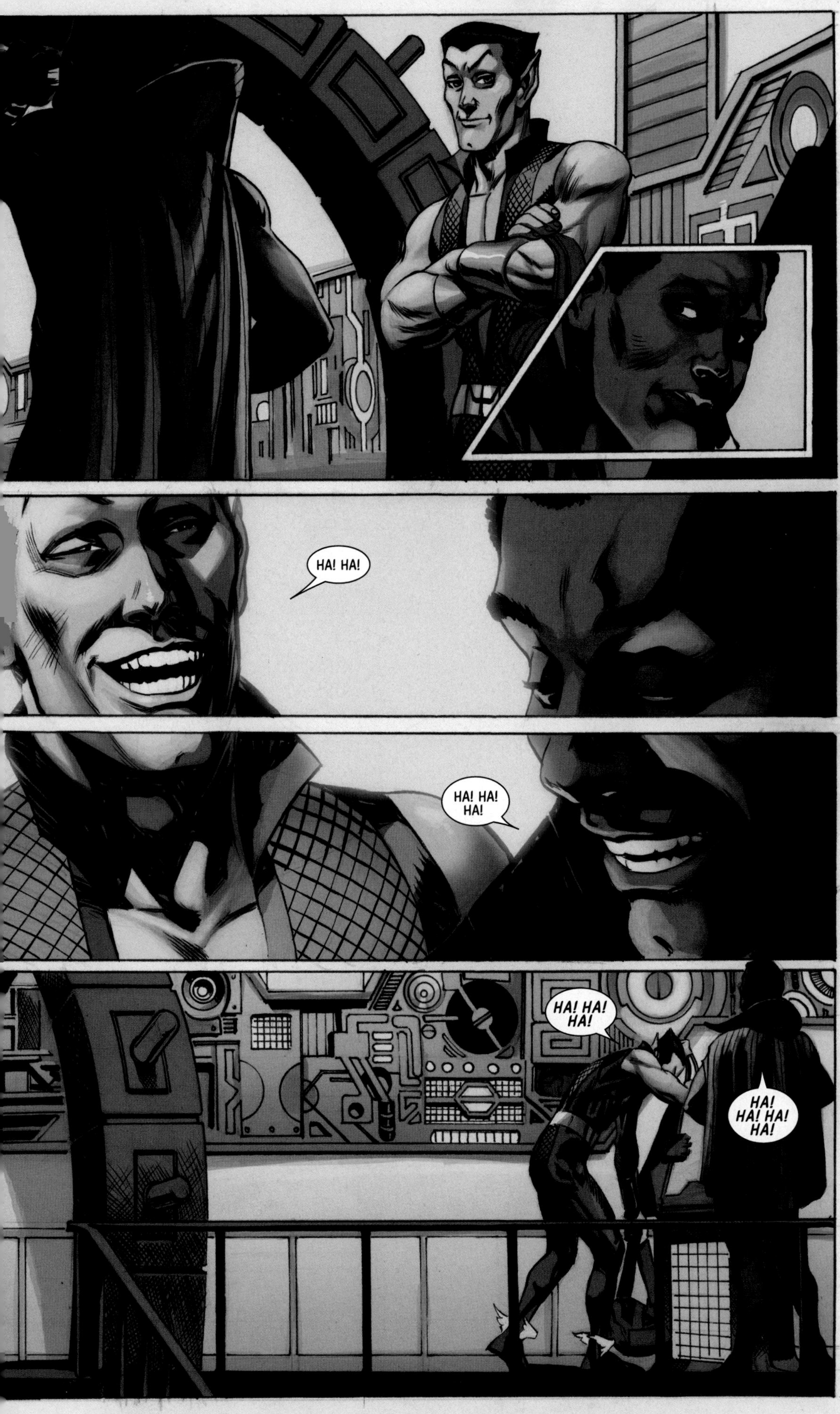
HA! HA!
HA! HA! HA!
HA! HA! HA!
HA! HA! HA! HA!

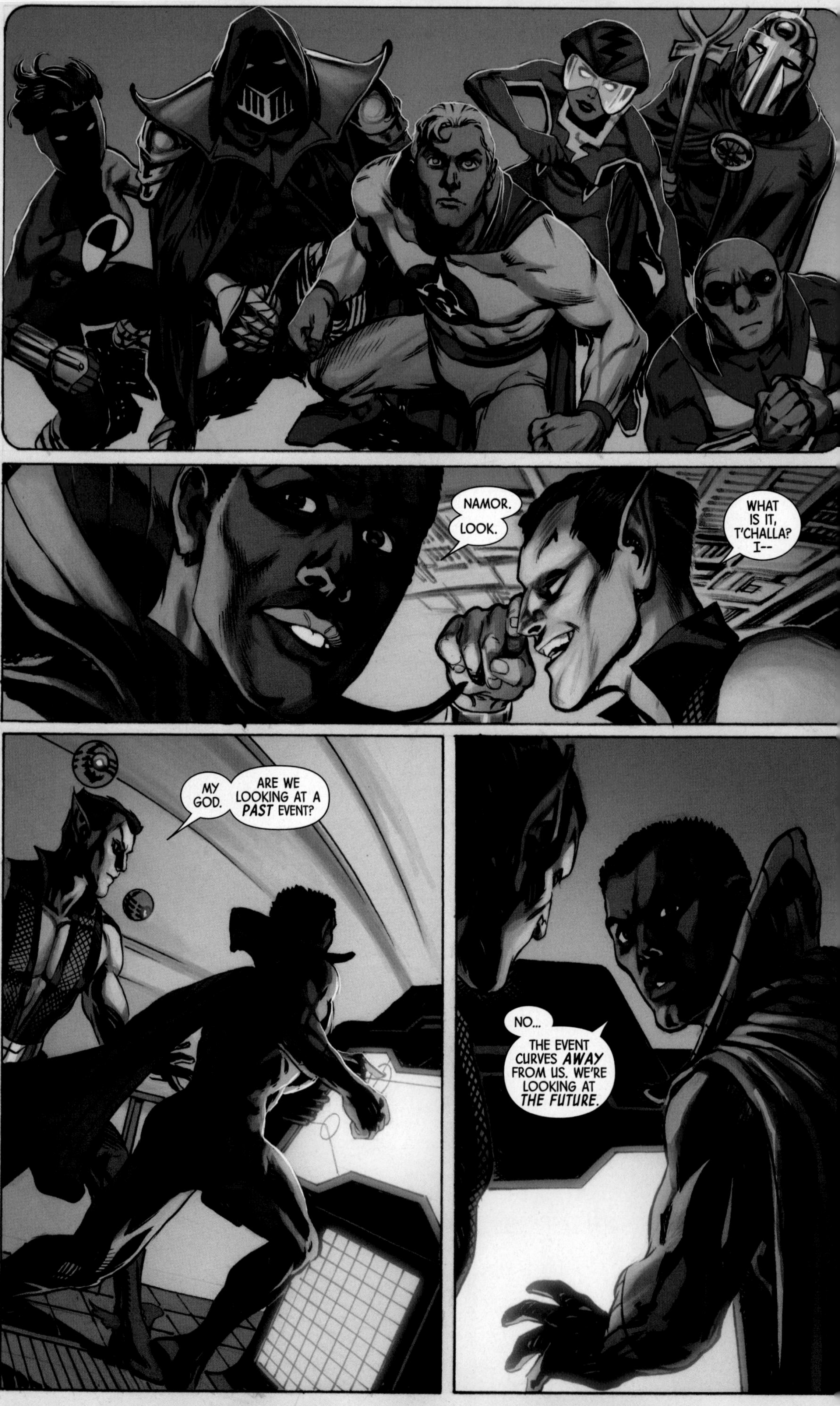
NAMOR.
LOOK.
WHAT IS IT, T'CHALLA? I--
MY GOD.
ARE WE LOOKING AT A *PAST* EVENT?
NO...
THE EVENT CURVES *AWAY* FROM US. WE'RE LOOKING AT *THE FUTURE*.

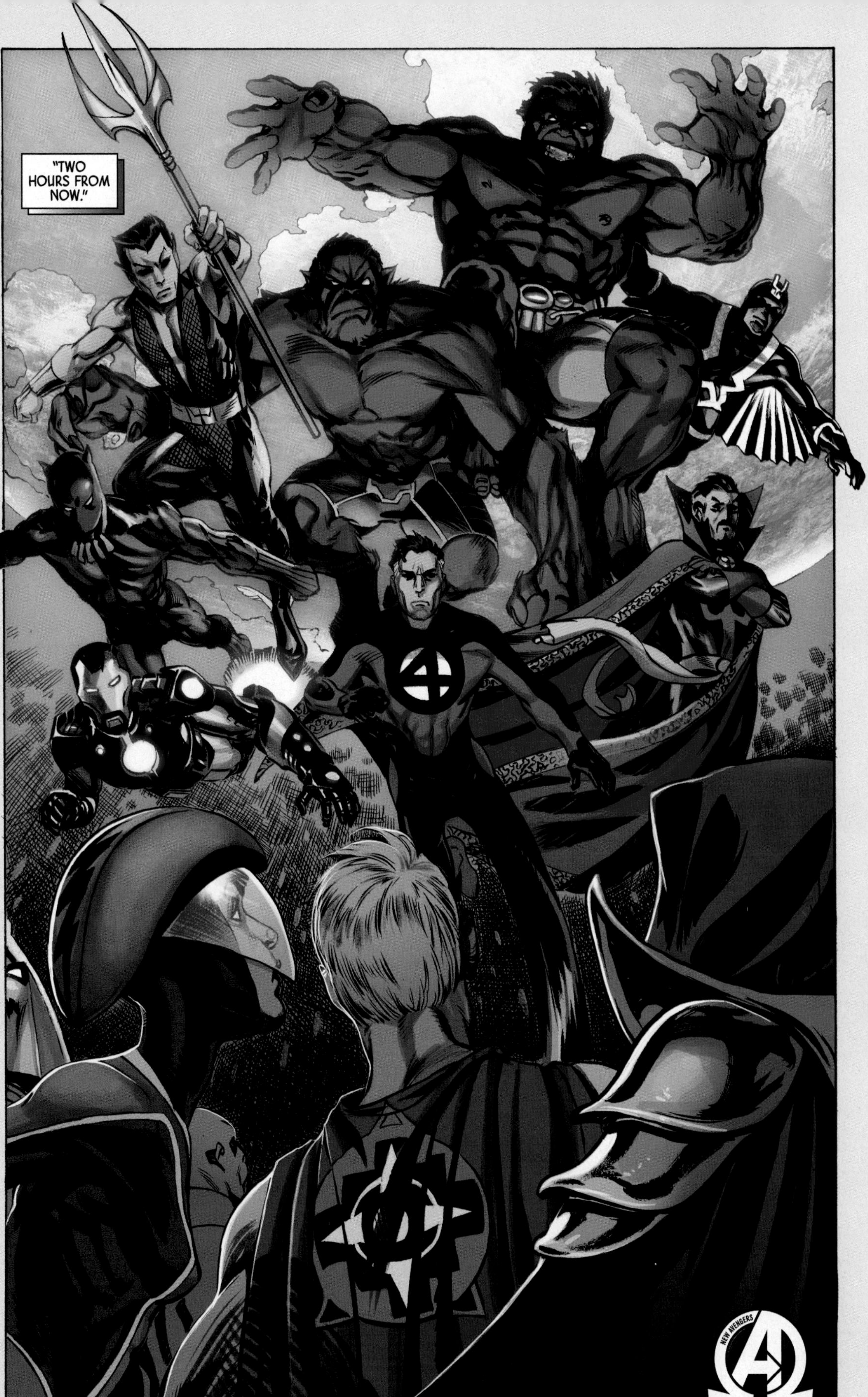
"TWO HOURS FROM NOW."
NEW AVENGERS

#13

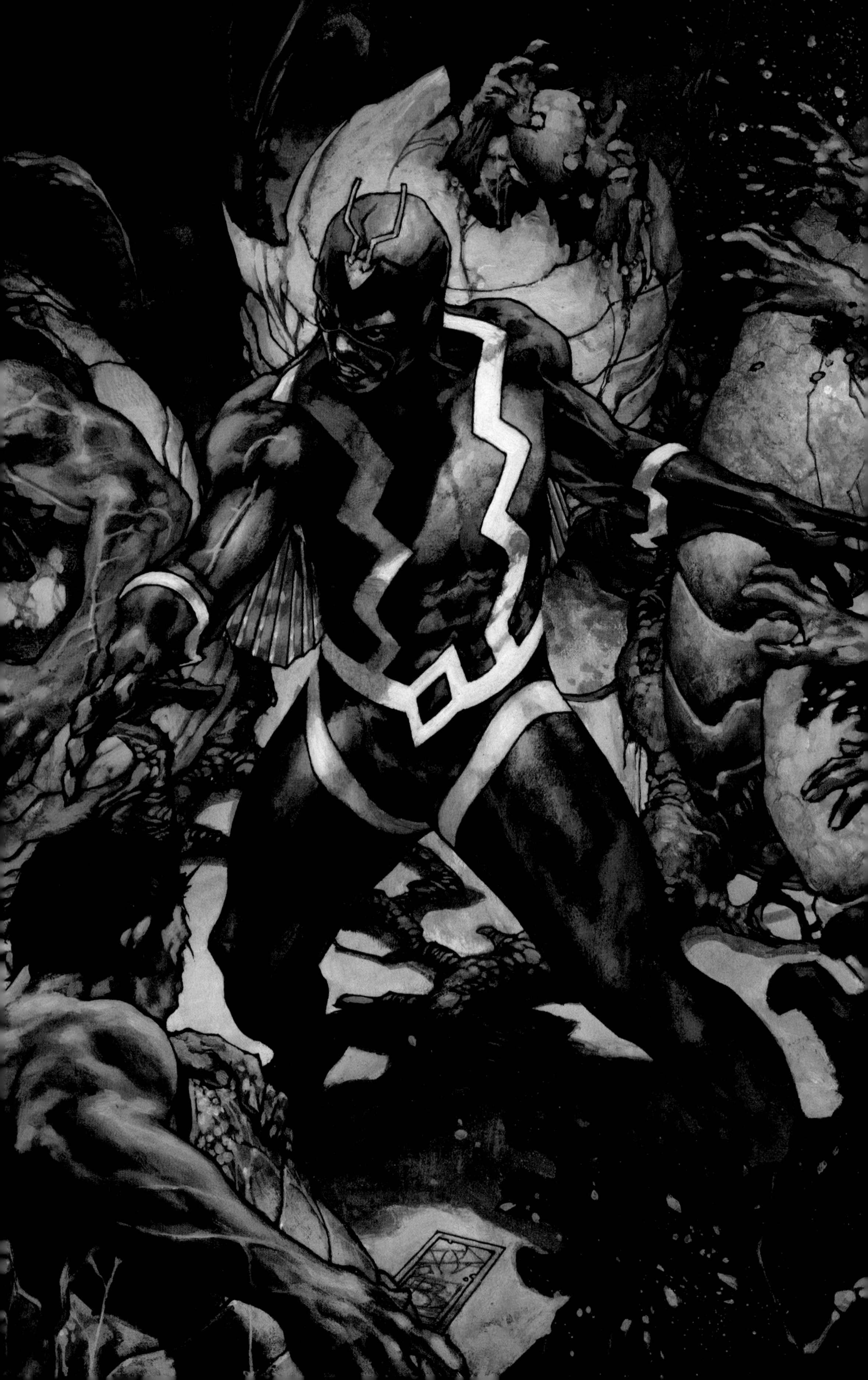

#14

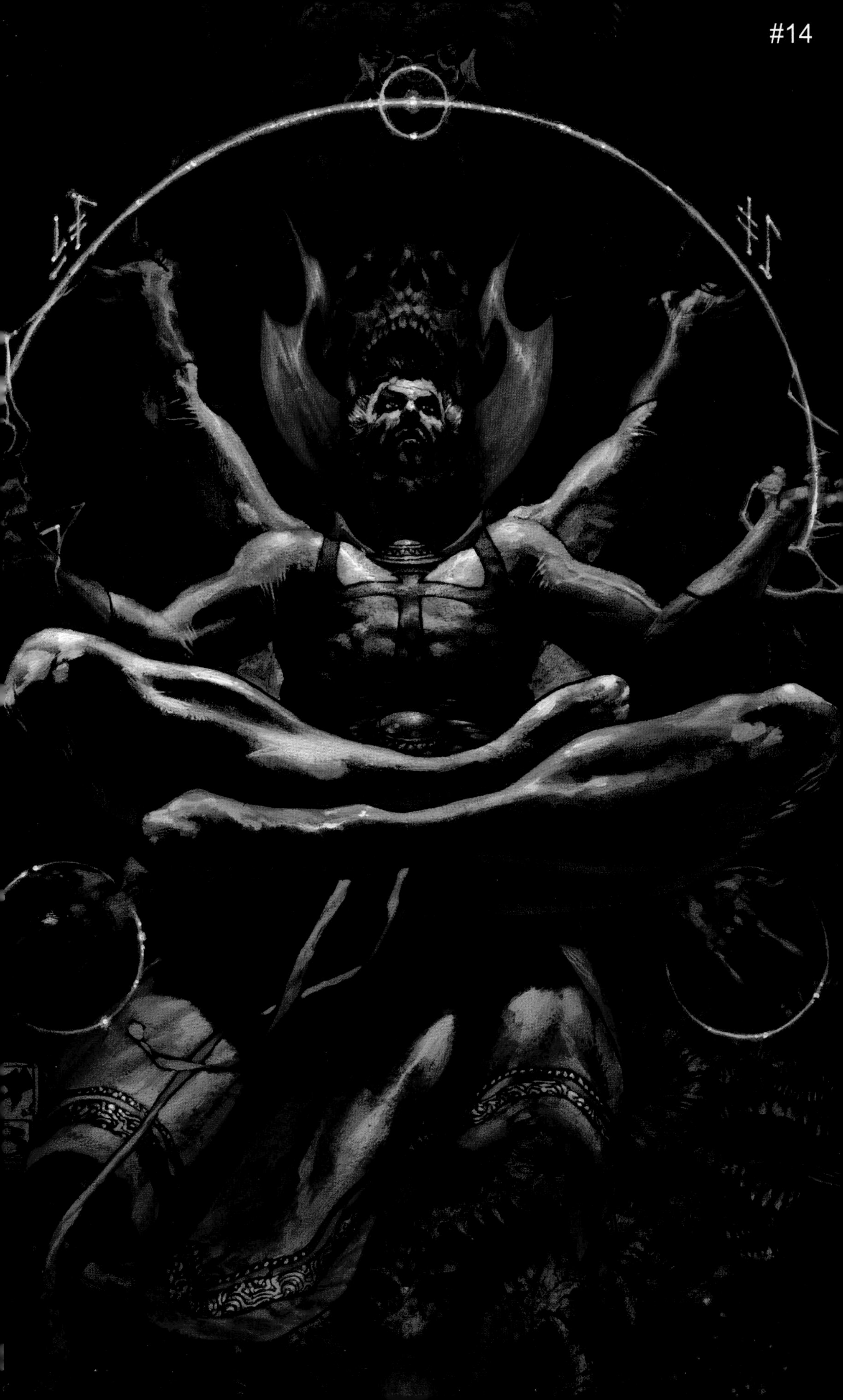

#15

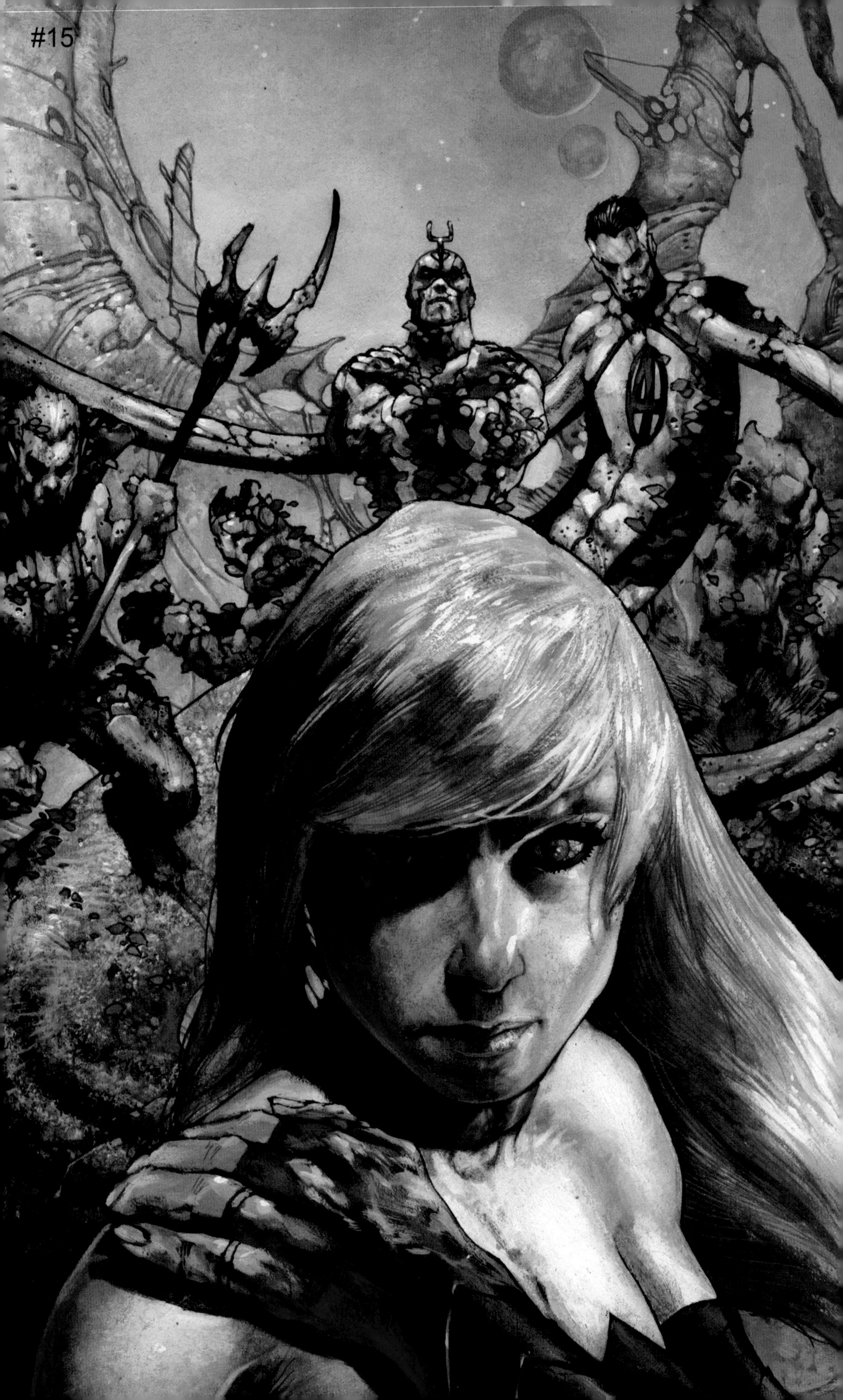

#16

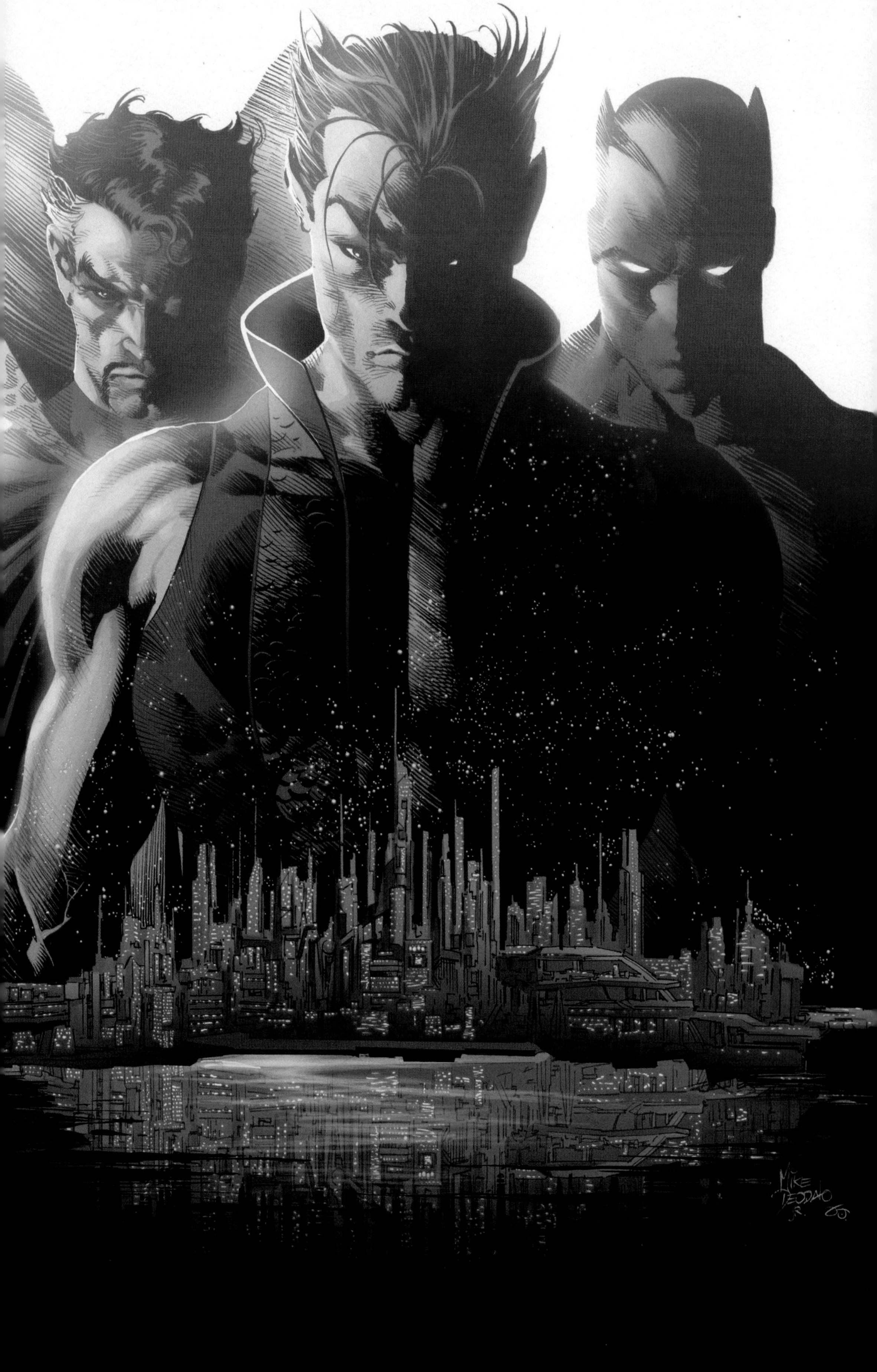

#17

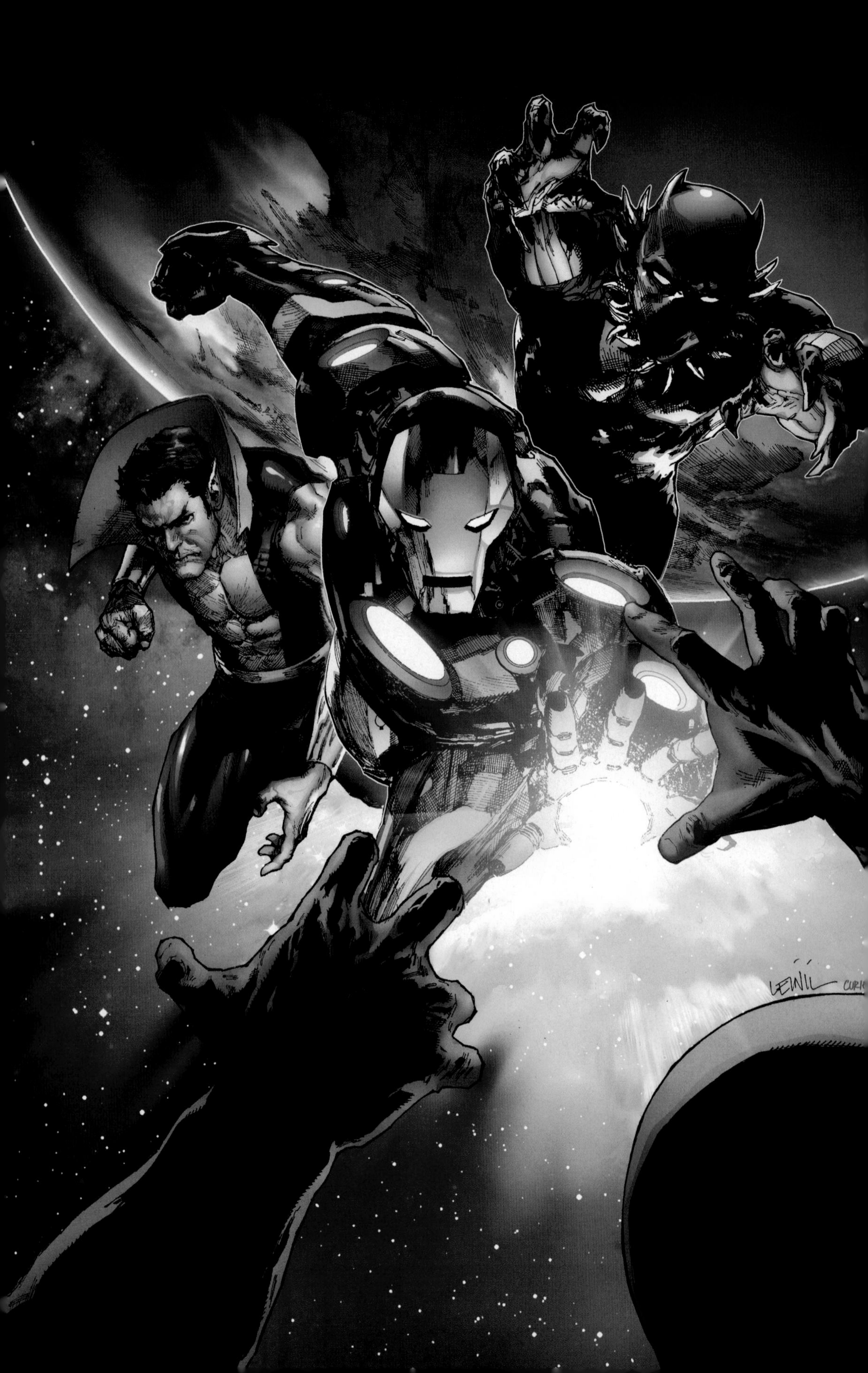

FINAL

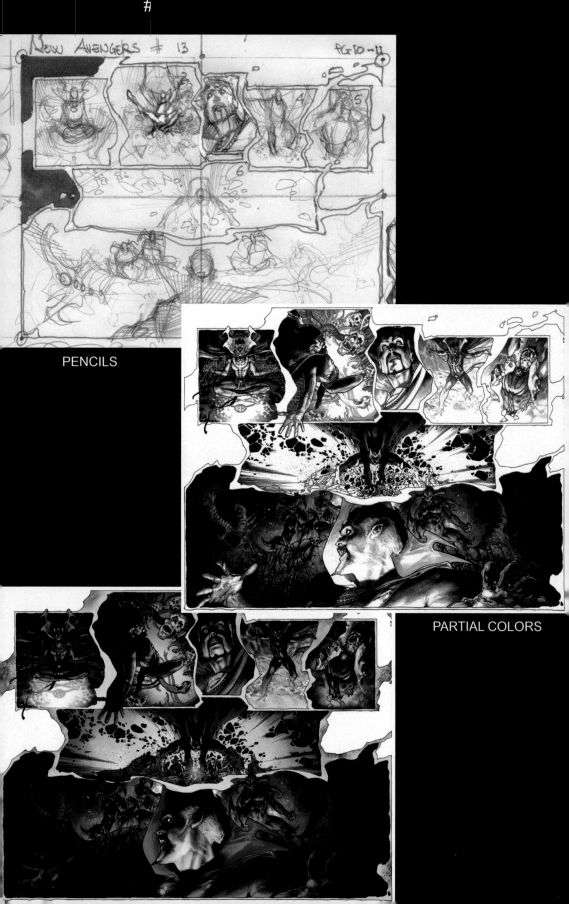

PENCILS

PARTIAL COLORS

#14 PENCILS BY **SIMONE BIANCHI**

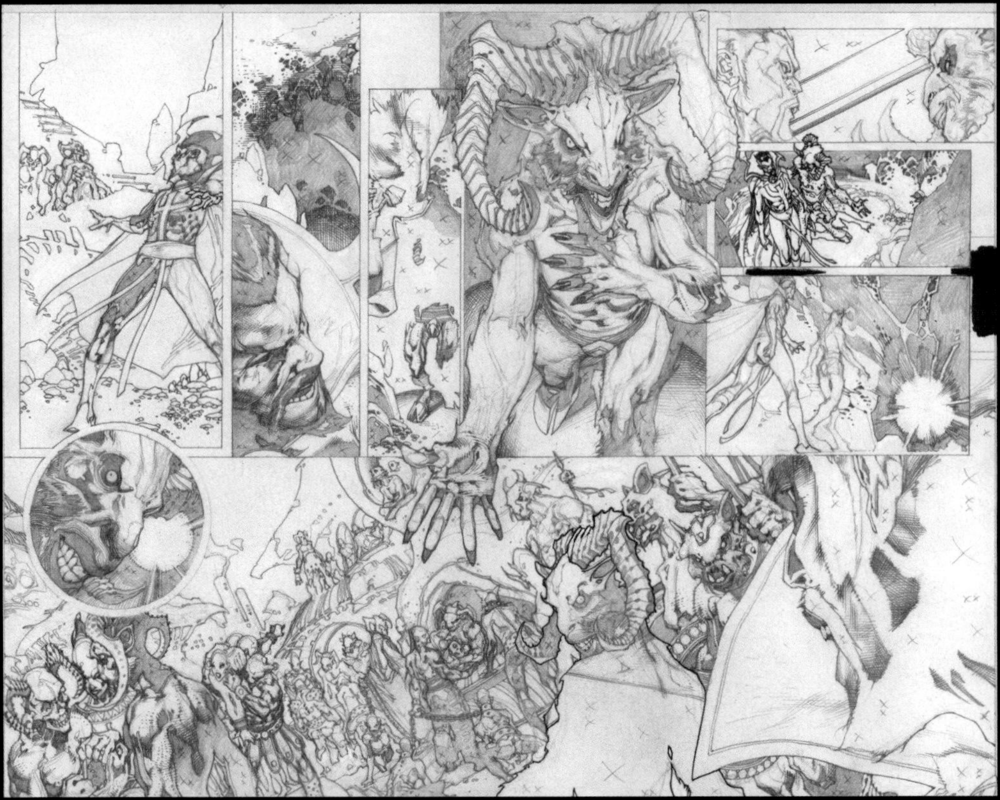

PAGES 6-7

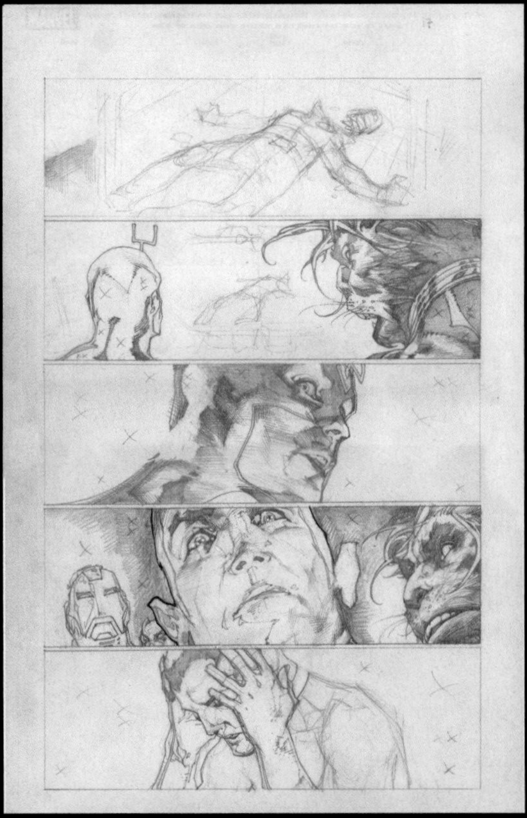

PAGE 16

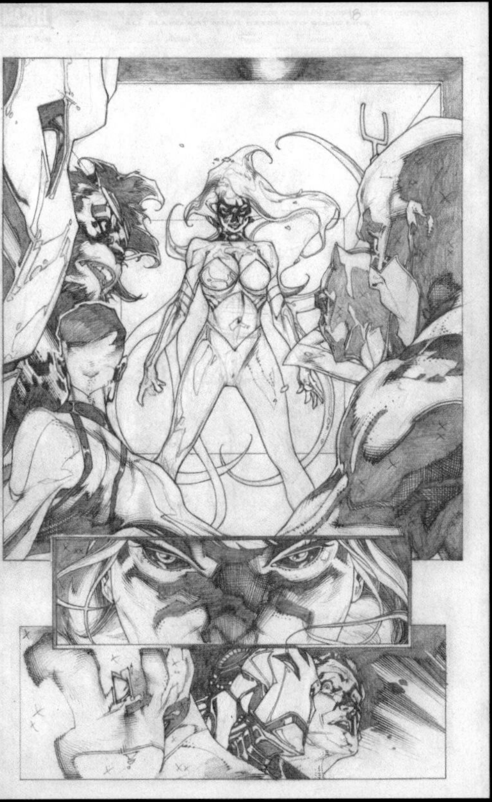

PAGE 18

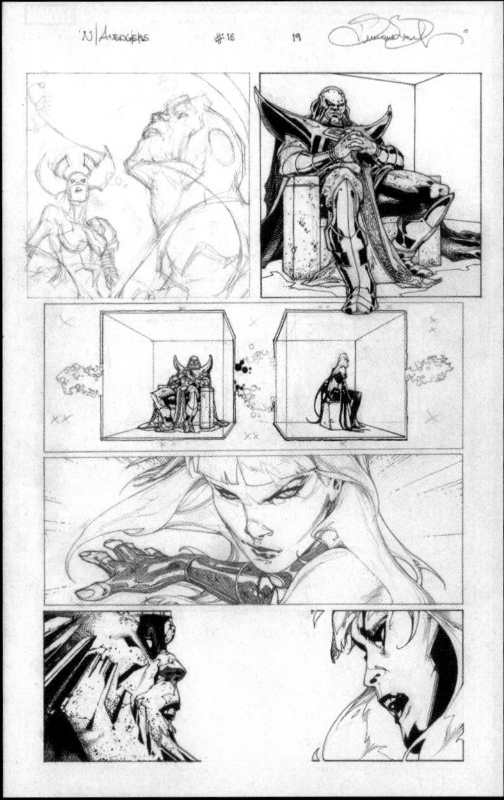
N/AVENGERS #16 19

PAGE 19

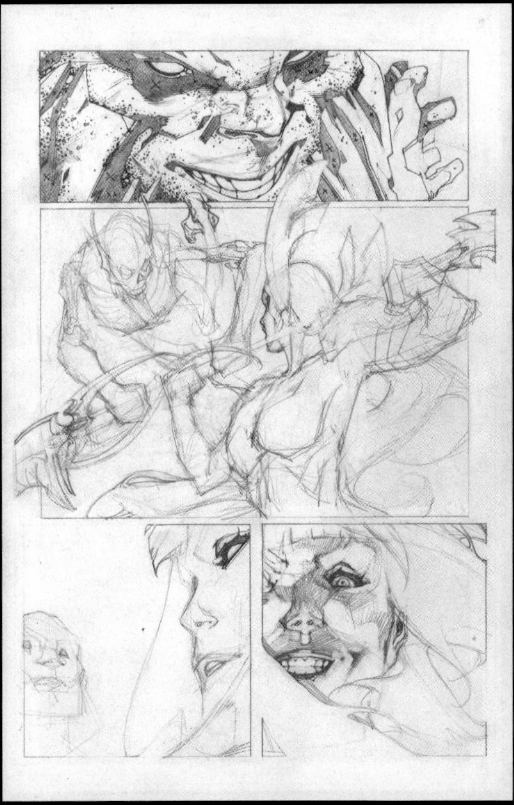

PAGE 20

#16 PAGE 6 PROCESS BY **RAGS MORALES**

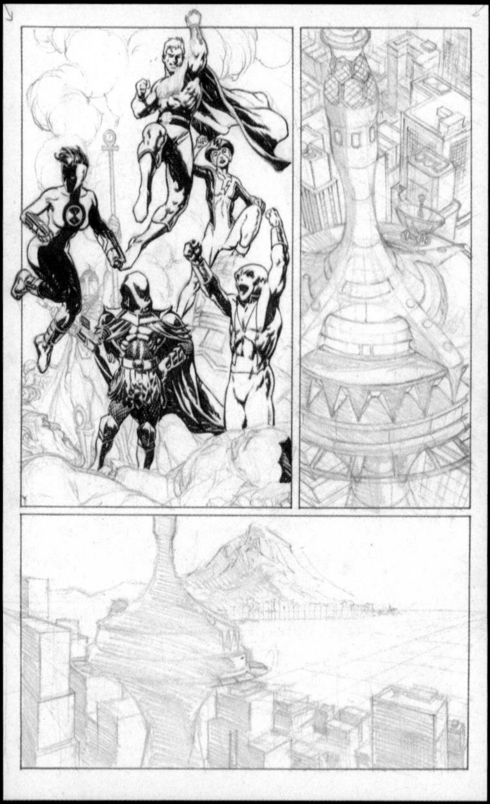

PENCILS

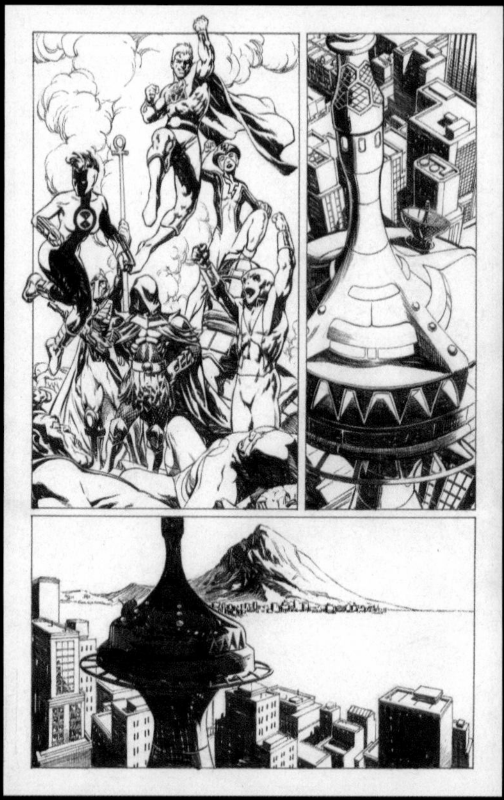

INKS

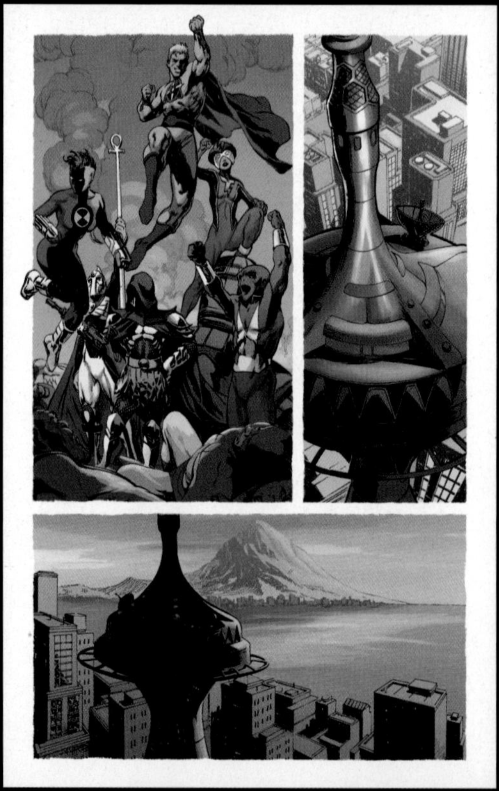

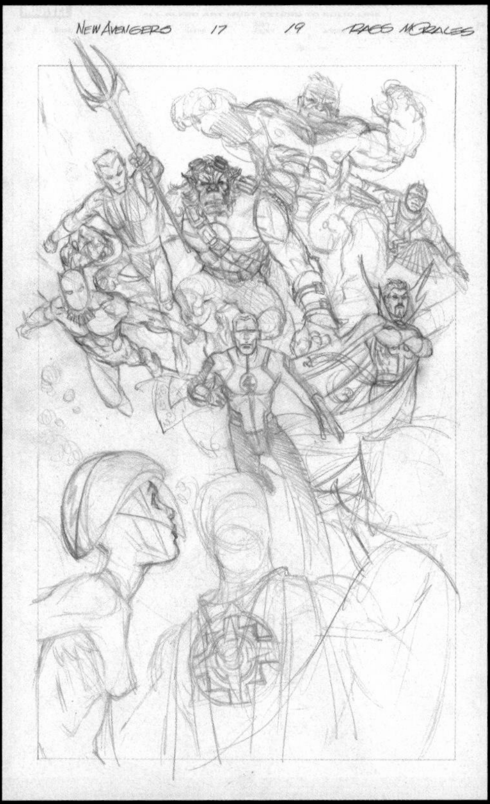
NEW AVENGERS 17 19 RAGS MORALES

PENCILS

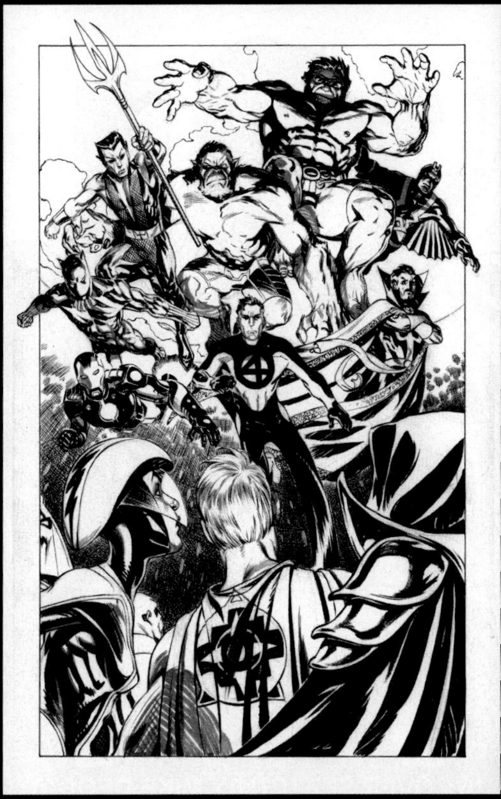

INKS

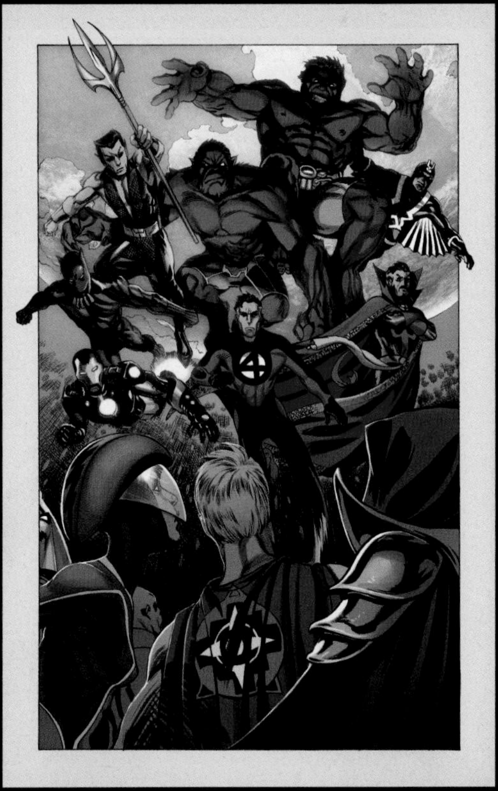

COLORS

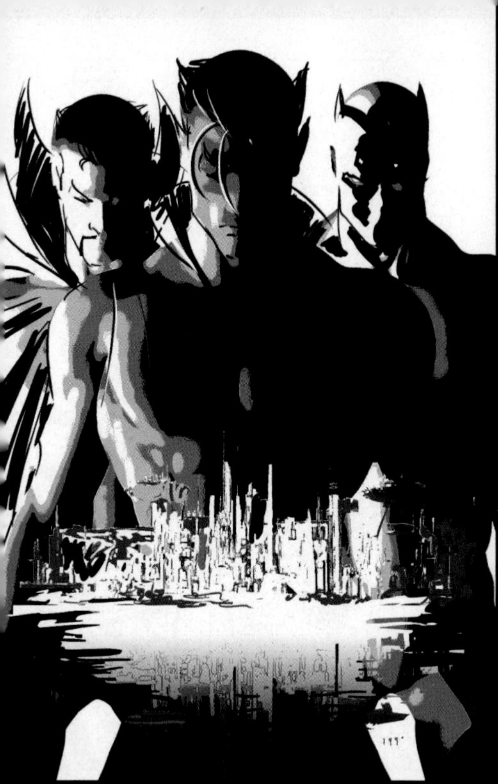

#16 COVER SKETCH BY **MIKE DEODATO**

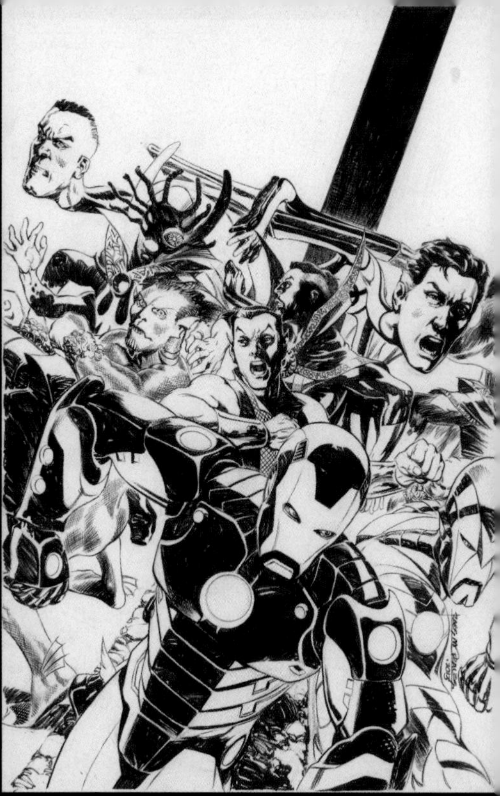

#16 VARIANT COVER INKS
BY **RAGS MORALES**

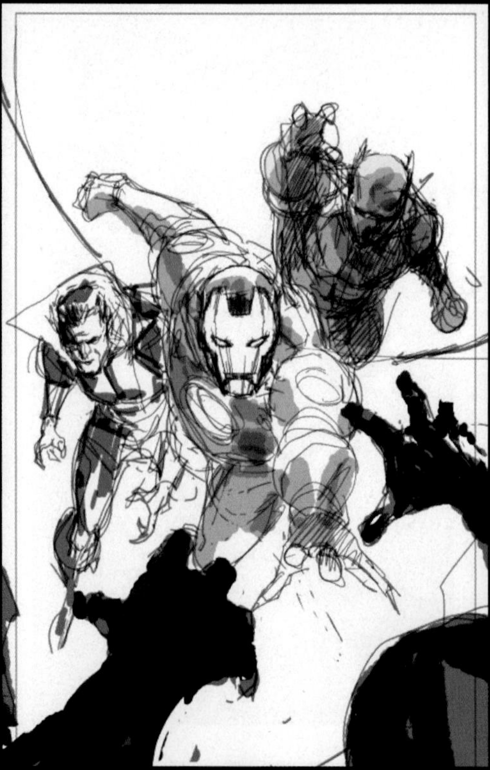

#17 COVER SKETCH BY **LEINIL YU**

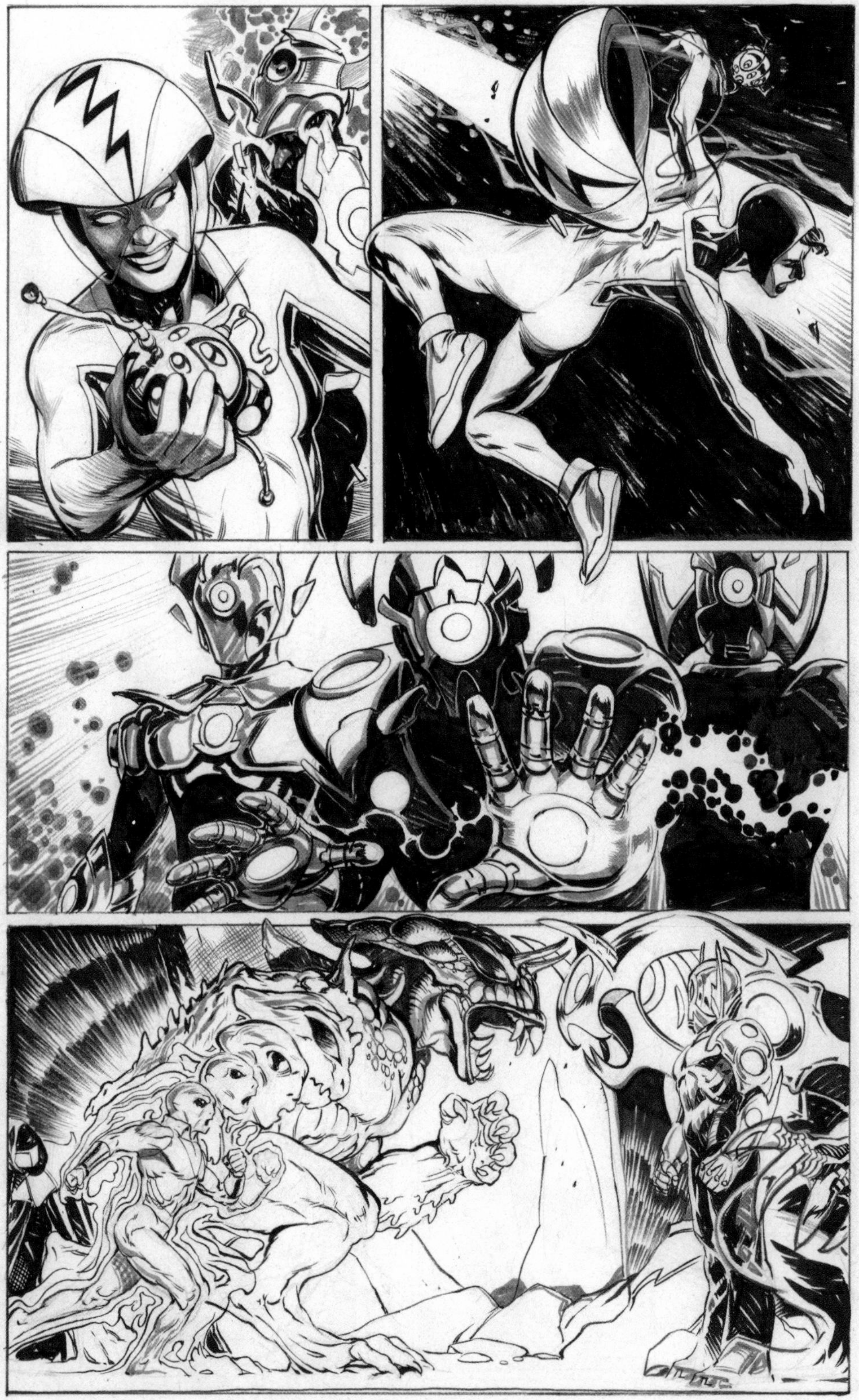

#17 PAGE 6 ART BY **RAGS MORALES**

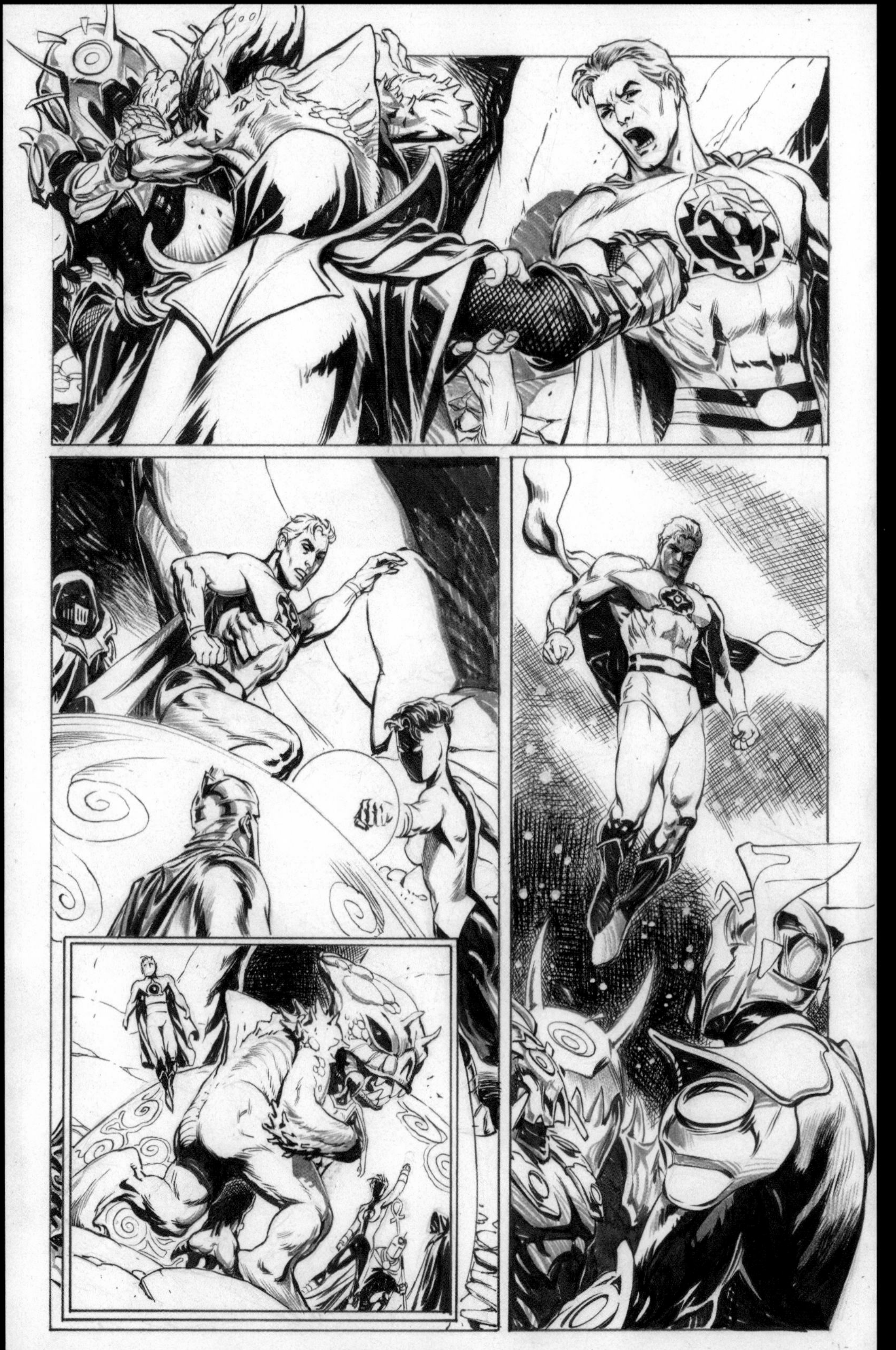

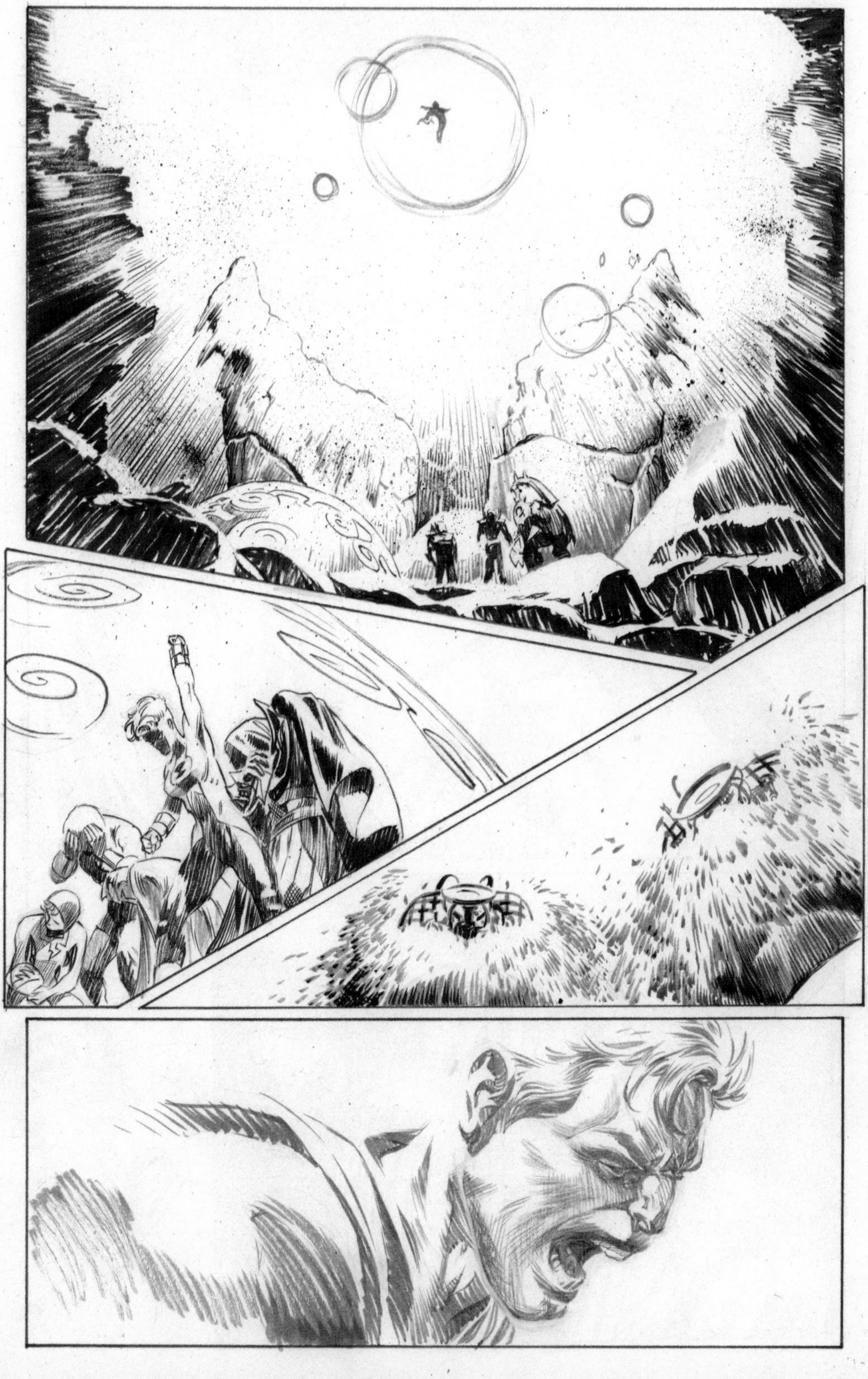

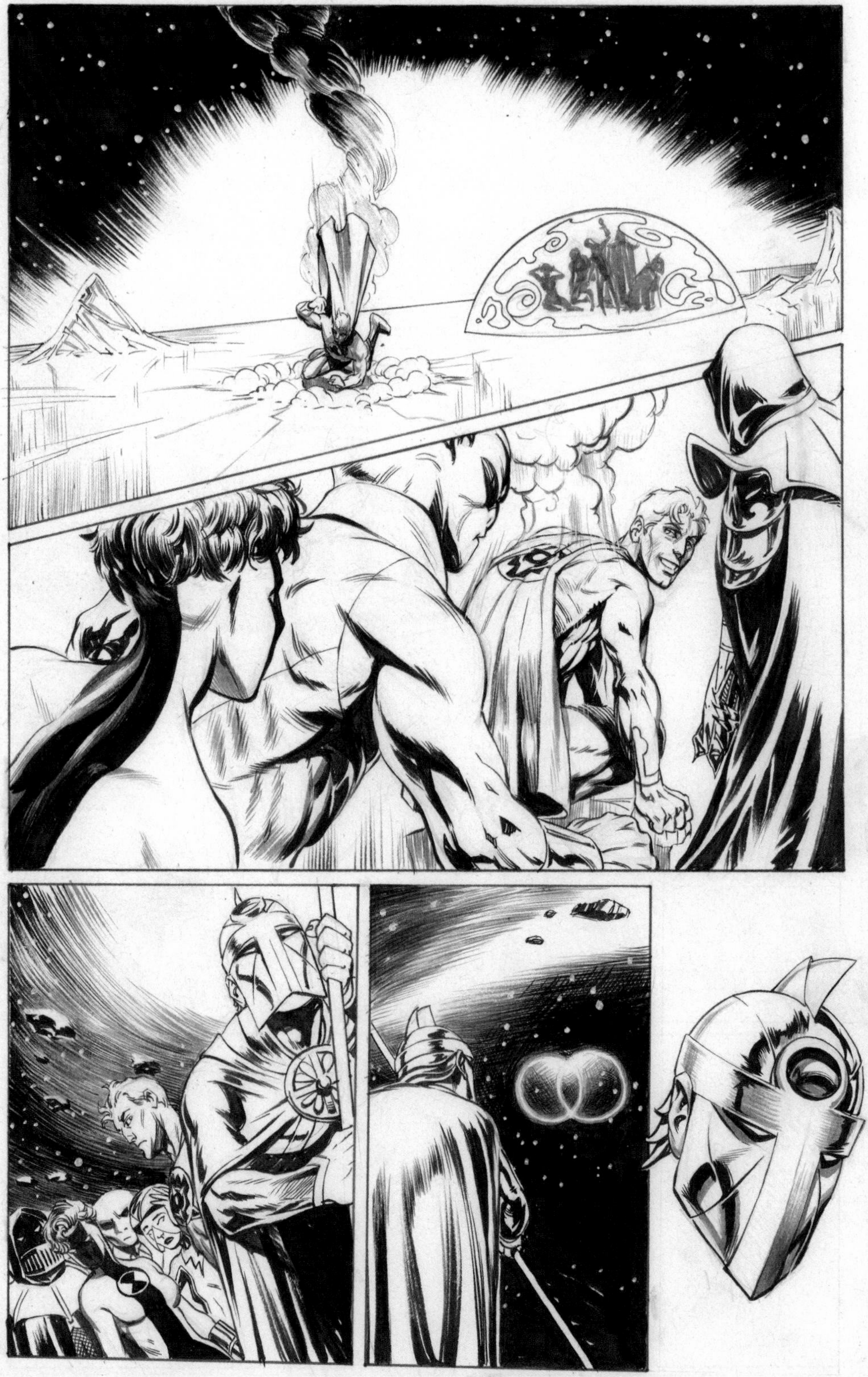

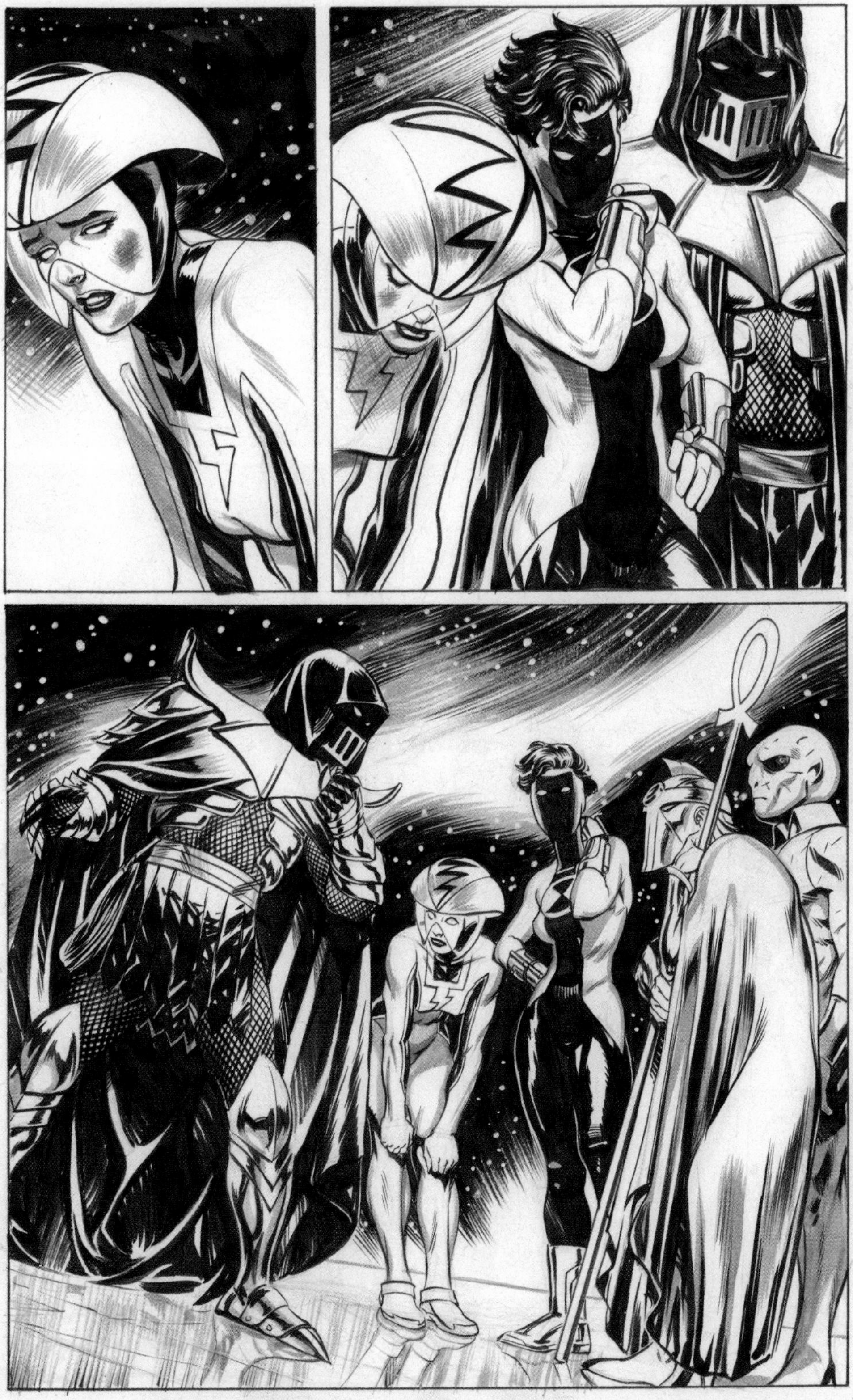

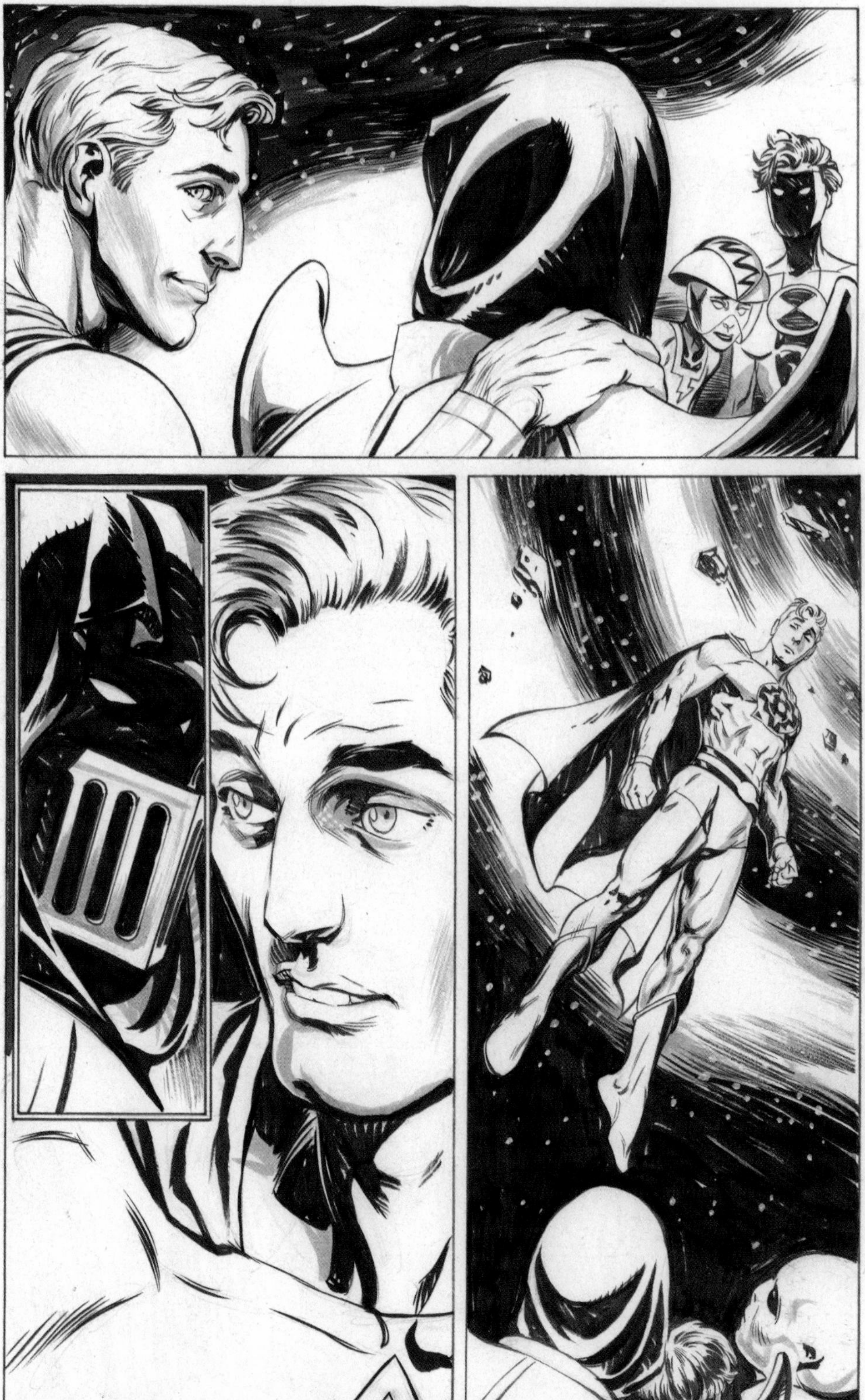

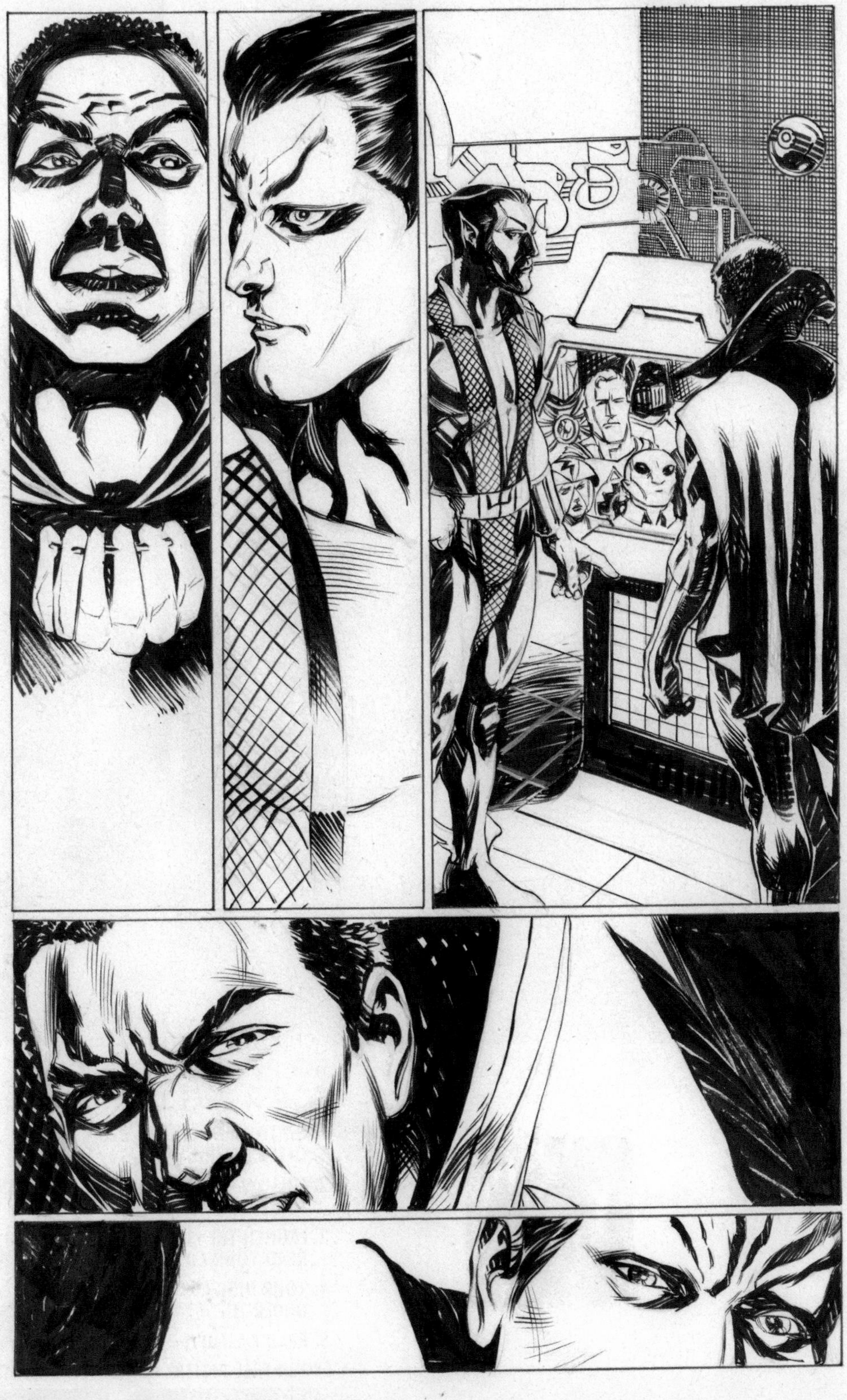